A HANDBOOK FOR THE PROSPECTIVE TEACHER

BRIJENDRA M. MATHUR
BEENA THADANI

ATLANTIC PUBLISHERS & DISTRIBUTORS
4215/1, Ansari Road, Darya Ganj
New Delhi-110002

Published by
Atlantic Publishers & Distributors
4215/1, Ansari Road, Darya Ganj,
New Delhi-110002

Head Office :
B-2, Vishal Enclave, Najafgarh Road
New Delhi-110027
Phone : 5413460

Printed at : Mohan Printing Corporation through
Chawla Composers, New Delhi

DEDICATED TO

The Memory of
Our Fathers
Whose Blessings
Are With Us For Ever

PREFACE

As we look towards twenty-first century, education assumes greater importance and has rightly been assigned higher priority by government as is clearly indicated by the National Education Policy, 1986. It is imperative, therefore, that the teachers in making should be properly equipped with knowledge and skills they are supposed to acquire in order to become successful in this grand task of nation building.

The present book is an effort in that direction. It makes the concepts of teaching and learning clear and deals with many topics which are essential for a progressive teacher to be known. It can serve as a text-book for the students of B. Ed. and M. Ed. of the Indian Universities as well as be a useful reference book for those who have already assumed the challenging task of teaching. Even an enlightened layman harbouring concern for education could be benefited by this book.

Beginning with the concepts of teaching and learning, it goes ahead to explaining the instructional strategies essential for effective teaching and the innovative practices which are yet to be introduced in most of the Indian schools. An effort has been made to include the things needed to equip a teacher for his profession. The concepts and methods of measurement and evaluation have been added. The elements of statistics useful in education have also found due place.

The authors do not claim originality, yet their analytical approach is expected to elicit the readers' interest in it. We are grateful to the educational thinkers and authors consulted in writing this book. We express our sincere thanks to Dr. K.R. Gupta of Atlantic Publishers & Distributors who has taken pains in bringing out the publication.

Bhilwara
11th, June 1988

BRIJENDRA M. MATHUR
BEENA THADANI

PREFACE

[illegible]

[illegible]

[illegible]

[illegible]

[illegible]

CONTENTS

1

CONCEPT OF TEACHING AND LEARNING

Teaching

The term 'teaching' clearly implies that the person who is engaged in the activity intends the students to learn something. The term 'teaching' also includes 'tasks' and 'achievement'. Thus 'teaching' can be defined as an activity aimed at the achievement of learning.

Teaching is a complex activity comprising many teaching acts. These acts can be easily divided into three categories. First, those acts which arise before teaching, secondly those acts that arise during teaching and thirdly, those acts which are to be taken into consideration after teaching. These acts are related to the kind of behaviour in which teacher engages in while working.

Before the teaching begins, the teacher is engaged in planning for teaching. He is engaged in selecting and arranging objects, developing learning activities, selecting teaching strategies, understanding learners, planning for motivation of students and designing evaluation procedures. Preparation for evaluation is done before teaching.

The teaching behaviours can be classified under the three categories:

1. Authoritarian teaching behaviours;
2. Democratic teaching behaviours; and
3. *Laissez faire* teaching behaviours.

1. *Authoritarian Teaching Behaviours*

This type of teaching behaviour is based on classical theory of organization task centred. In this type of behaviour, the teacher plays a dominant role. He/she directs the students and plans and performs each and every activity of the class. Thus in this behaviour teacher is active while students are passive listeners.

H.C. Morrison has defined 'teaching' according to authoritarian mode of behaviour : Teaching is an intimate contact between a more mature personality and a less mature which is designed to further the education of the latter. In this definition Morrison considers that teacher is a more mature personality and student is less mature personality. He has given primary place to the teacher while secondary place to the students.

In authoritarian teaching there is no place of feelings and attitudes of the students and this type of teaching confines to memory level only.

2. *Democratic Teaching Behaviours*

This type of teaching behaviour is based on 'Human relations theory of organization relationship centred.' In this behaviour students are motivated by teacher so they are free to participate in the system of organization behaviour. Edmund Amidon (1967) has defined the term 'teaching' in view of the democratic mode of behaviour:

"Teaching is defined as an interactive process, primarily involving classroom talk which takes place between teacher and pupils and occurs during definable activities."

Amidon considers teaching as an interactive process.

Ned A. Flanders defines "teaching" as an interactive process. Interaction means participation of both teacher and students and both are benefited by this. The interaction takes place for achieving desired objectives.

N.L. Gage also defines according to the democratic mode of behaviour:

"Teaching is a form of interpersonal relationship between teacher and students. The objectives of teaching is to change the behaviours of the students.

In this type of behaviour interchange of ideas, evidence occur in between teacher and students.

3. Laissez Faire *Teaching Behaviours*

This teaching behaviour is based on Modern theory of organization: Task and relationship centred.

In Laissez Faire teaching behaviour the students are more active than the teacher. Teacher creates situation for students and students find place where problem lie. Thus teacher opens a field of investigation.

Here students decide what they want to do and how they will do it. Thus this type of teaching is related with reflective thinking.

John Brubacher has defined the term teaching according to to the laissez faire mode of behaviour:

"Teaching is an arrangement and manipulation of a situation in which there are gaps and obstructions which an individual will seek to overcome and from which he will learn in the course of doing so."

B.O. Smith has defined the term teaching as follows:

"Teaching as a system of actions intends to induce learning through interpersonal relationships."

According to this definition interpersonal relationships are essential in teaching which influence learning. These relationships vary from situation to situation.

Teaching Variables

Teaching process involves three variables:

1. Independent variable is the teacher.
2. Dependent variable is the student.
3. Intervening variables are the content and strategy of presentation.

1. The teacher plays a role of independent variable in teaching. He/she plans, organizes and controls the teaching activities. He/she also provides learning experiences to the pupils.
2. In the process of teaching student plays a role of dependent variable because student has to act according to the planning and organization of the teacher. Perfor-

mance of student is directly influenced by activities of the teacher.

3. The content of teaching, strategy, tactics of teaching and techniques of motivation are known as intervening variables. The interaction between teacher and student is performed through the intervening variables. The content determines the mode of presentation– telling, showing and doing.

Nature of Teaching

There are three focal points in education—the teacher, child and the subject. Teaching, in the first place, is a relationship with which is established between these three, or 'teaching' brings all teacher, child and subject into a relationship. *Thus teaching is the process by which that adult brings that child and that subject together.*

All three 'elements' as we may call them, have their place in the relationship. We cannot have 'teaching' without all three being present. But the position of the norms, the teachers is an active agent in the process of establishing and developing the relationship, when we consider the nature of learning, that the child is also very active. But when we learn at the process of education from the point of view of teaching then we are considering the characteristic activity of the teacher. He actively 'teaches' his pupils. While we are considering the nature of teaching we are concerned with the activity of the teacher. When we consider the nature of learning we are concerned with the pupil's activity.

Teaching is giving information. It is exposition. When a teacher is teaching he is often giving new information to his children. This one essential part of teaching is communicating knowledge.

But, important as it is, the giving of information is not the most essential aspect of teaching. Still, more important is the fact that teaching is 'causing to learn'. The most fundamental principle of *teaching is that teaching means helping a child to learn and to do things himself.* The teacher therefore is an instrument. He is there to cause learning, to help development, to enable the child to establish his own relationship with his subject and his environment. *Teaching* from this point of view is a *matter of helping the child to respond to his environment in an effective way.* Thus teaching is helping a child to adjust himself to his environment.

A major part of the work of teaching is to provide opportunities for the exercise of this desire, for activity and to give children the encouragement which will help them to use that tendency to be active in helpful and fruitful ways.

But while it is true that children like to be active and to do things themselves, we must never lose sight of the fact that they need guidance and need it right through their school course. *Teaching is not only encouragement, it is also guidance in the exercise of the activity which has been aroused.*

While teaching means the providing of opportunities for the child to exercise its desire to be active, it further includes the training of the 'emotions of the child'. Action depends on feeling. If we wish for right action we must secure right feeling. If we wish for right development we must help children to develop interests in worthwhile things. *Thus teaching is not simply a matter of encouraging and developing the mental and physical powers of the child. It is also the encouraging and training of the emotional life.* Good teaching should enable children to develop emotional stability. When the emotion loses its strength, the whole personality of the child suffers.

It is not simply action that it required, but action along worthwhile lines. In other words we have to guide our pupils into such activities as will sublimate their instinctive urges to action, and will help them to organize their instincts with the attached emotions sound worthwhile centres to form worthy sentiments. It is this organization sentiments that is one of the great tasks of teaching on which the whole formation of character depends. As the emotions are attached to good objects, so are they trained and so its the character formed. Hence from this point of view "*teaching is a matter of doing what one can to enable sublimation to take place in the gradually developing lives of those who are being taught.*"

Teaching is largely a matter of suggestion. Suggestions are continually flowing from the personality and example of the teacher to his children. The ideals, the habits, the actions, the words of the teacher are all having their effect on his children, and often his real teaching goes on without his being aware of what is being done. The late President Eliot of Harvard once said, "The supreme value of a teacher lies not in the regular performance of routine duties, but in his power to lead and inspire his student through the influence of his own mental and moral personality and example."

Thus teaching is both a conscious and an unconscious process and the most effective part of it is quite often the part of which we are unconscious.

Teaching, while considering the matter of adjustment, is something which helps the child to prepare for life after school days are over. Thus teaching is a means of preparation.

Characteristics of teaching

1. Teaching is a set of acts, designed and organized to induce learning.
2. Teaching is a rational process.
3. Teaching is a behaviour and is subject to observation, analysis, improvement and change.
4. Teacher can learn to observe, analyze, control and improve his "teaching behaviours".
5. Teaching is an intended interaction between teacher and the learners to help them to achieve their potential.
6. Teaching involves proper planning, effective approaches, relevant content and evaluation procedure.
7. Teaching includes pre-interactive phase, interactive phase and post-interactive phase.
8. Teaching is an interactive process and demands mastery over teaching skills.

Teaching is an Act

The acts of teaching are many; such acts are informing, explaining, describing, exemplying etc. There is another category of acts which is concerned with controlling, motivating and evaluating. This type of acts are managerial in nature and are supportive to the intellectual acts which take place when interaction between the teacher and pupils is going on.

Different phases of teaching

Classroom teaching has two phases that is, interactive and non-interactive. In the interactive phase, the teacher is engaged in social interaction. In this situation, teacher provides stimulus to get response from the students. Thus there is give and take of social interaction when, the learner is actually face to face with his students. In the non-interactive phase, teacher works alone or in terms to prepare for the interactive phase. In this phase teachers do planning and preparation for teaching. Thus it is useful to divide teaching into three phases which are as follows:

(a) *Pre-interactive phase*: This phase is generally utilized on lesson planning, collecting and preparation of teaching aids, preparing tests for evaluation and preparation of assignments etc.

(b) *The Interactive phase*: This phase is related directly to the interaction between teacher and students in the classroom. It includes acts of teaching which are essential for generating learning as well as for controlling the class. It is related to the desirable teacher behaviour in the classroom which influence imitation, organization, teacher directions or teacher talk. It is also related to teacher questions, students responses and providing positive reinforcement.

(c) *The Post-interactive phase*: In this phase the teacher tries to get feed-back about his teaching which helps him in replan and reteach effectively. This is the phase when a teacher can observe his teaching, evaluate his teaching and can improve it. This phase clearly indicates in the performance of the teacher.

Characteristics of Good Teaching

The characteristics of good teaching are given below:

1. Good teaching requires appropriate responsiveness to the dates and child and group are placing in the situation. The child activities can be rewarded properly.
2. Good teaching requires a reduction in the controlling functions exercised continuously by the teacher. Teacher behaviour should be indirect. Flanders found in his study that the indirectness in teacher who goes alongwith greater achievement on the part of their pupils.
3. Good teaching requires that the classroom be well managed so that the business of learning may receive full attention. Teachers perform the functions of controlling with clarity and with consistency.
4. Good teaching requires that the human environment be

acceptable to each individual; that in some way it impresses upon him that he is important. It suggests a personal rapport between teacher and students.

5. Good teaching helps or maintains the interpersonal relationships, supportive within the classroom out of which a shared problem solving attitude develops.
6. Good teaching requires that the teacher be a well educated mature person who has the insight and energy for this demanding job. It requires the responsive human environment and fosters exploration and initiative.

How to Improve on teaching?

Since teaching has been accepted as an act of behaviour which is observable, can also be analysed then it is possible to reinforce weak points and new skills can be mastered. Teaching improvement is possible through practice based on proper feed-back. It also depends on a "feeling of need to change" or "positive attitude towards change".

Training is essential for a teacher to sharpen teaching skills. One should always remember that professionalism in teaching requires a life-long commitment to improve.

Learning

Every animal in this world is born with a certain number of innate dispositions, which determine its initial responses. These initial responses enable it to adopt itself to the simple environment which is around it. But man lives in a complex environment and so these innate grades of behaviour are inadequate for his adaptation to the environment. He has to profit by experience or learn to make his responses more suitable to the environment. In this sense, we may call learning as the process of acquiring the appropriate responses. When the child begins to learn, his learning is crude and exploratory in nature. At this stage, the child's actions are undifferentiated and often his responses are wrong. With proper training the child learns to reduce his errors, brings co-ordination in his efforts and the state of uncertainty is replaced by that of decision. Child grows old, there is brought order out of confusion and he learns to perform his tasks with ease.

We mean by referring to "the improvement in the individual" and saying that thus "learning is profiting by experience", that learning is not merely the acquisition of facts and skills through mechanized procedures, such as, repititive practice. In learning, the learner learns to organize and evaluate the learning materials, endows them with many meanings and interpretations and becomes conscious of working towards goals.

Definition of Learning

Bernhardt defines learning as "the more or less permanent modification of an individual's activity in a given situation, due to practice in attempts to achieve some goal or solve some problem". Learning is an active process which depends on the activity of the individual himself. On the other hand, the process of natural growth, or maturation, is a process of development with which the individual himself has little to do.

"Learning is modification of behaviour through experience" what a man learns is determined, on the one hand, by his constitution, and on the other, by the demands which the environment makes upon him. Man is influenced much by the environment. He is flexible in his attitude. "He inherits only a few fixed ways of reacting. His interests, attitude, appreciations, skills and abilities are primarily the product of learning."

In the opinion of Peel, "Learning is a change in the individual following upon changes in his environment." Peel, however, emphasizes that each and every change in the environment is not learning. If a person falls unconscious in a motor accident, then it is not learning.

Peel summarizes learning as follows :

(i) Learning is not a reflex action. It means that writing or withdrawal of leg when knee is struck is not learning. There are psychological actions which a person automatically performs.

(ii) Learning may be for conscious pusposes or it may be for biological and social adjustment.

(iii) Through learning, in a person permanent or temporary changes are produced.

(iv) It can be for adjustment or maladjustment. It can create a socially-adjusted individual or it may give rise to anti-social behaviour.

Characteristics of learning

1. Learning requires interaction with some activity, situation, person or thinking.
2. Learning requires internal information processing.
3. Learning is related to the behaviour of the individual.
4. Learning occurs everywhere on varied forms.
5. Learning is continuous process. It continues for whole of the life.
6. Learning is positive as well as negative.
7. Learning is varied in nature. There are many forms of learning which are related to different theories of learning.
8. Learning is a social process.
9. Learning is a process of adjustment.
10. Learning is a rational activity.
11. Learning is a process of solving a problem.

The Learning Process

In its simplest stages learning is a matter of making a response to a situation or modifying a previous response in order to bring about an improvement. He may do this through a process of trial and error, or he may use his powers of thinking to correct himself. But as a result of his trials he finds the best response or way of acting, and then concentrates on that, that is, he repeats that particular action. Then we say that he is learning the right way to act in this particular situation. Thus learning is first selection and then practice.

For example, a child learns to read. He comes to a word he does not know. He makes several responses, that is, says several words before he gets the right one. Then when he gets the right one he probably practises it several times. He selects and then practises. He selects the one which gives him satisfaction, that is, which helps him to carry out his purpose. Thus learning has been a matter of selection of the response to a situation, which gives the best results.

In all those parts of life where we take advantages of habit, learning will result in a particular response always being made to a particular situation until it is made without our thinking about it. When a child first learns to put on his own clothes he has to think about it, he makes mistakes and has, sometimes to take things off and put them on again. But gradually, as he learns the right response, that is, learns to do things in the right way, his actions, we say, become habitual. This simply means that the right response follows the stimulus without his having to think about it. Finally he makes the response to the stimulus while he is thinking about something else altogether. Thus in all things where habits are to be formed it is very important to help the child to select the right response from the very beginning. Learning takes place in the following ways:

1. *Stimulation*: The situation in which the child finds himself in some way rouses the desire to act in a particular way he is interested. He feels that urge to use his instinctive energy in some particular way. For instance the boy wants to make a boat. His creative urge has been aroused. In some way or other his environment has given him a stimulus.

2. *Selection*: The stimulation rouses to action, and this may take many forms. These are the responses. The child then selects what seems the best or most hopeful response, that is, the response which looks as if it would help him to do what he wants to do.

3. *Action*: Having selected his response, that is, his line of action, he has then to act. He must do something. He can never learn to make a boat by sitting and listening to his teacher, telling him how to do it. His teacher may help him to decide on what response to make but the child must act himself.

4. *Re-consideration of Response*: The child may find the response he makes is not as fruitful as he thought it would be. His selection has not been right. His action tells him this. So he then reconsiders his selection in the light of the experience he has got, and makes a new selection. A new action ensues, until he is sure he has the right response. The teacher's help will all along be available to him as he sets himself right.

5. *Habit*: Finally after much practice, a habit is formed, and the child can perform the skill without effort and without thinking about it. It may be, of course, that his habit is not very good one. In other words the degree of skill he has attained is not a very high one. If not watched carefully by the teacher he may also have made wrong responses habitual. The whole process has then to be gone over again, but it is obvious how much more difficult it is to correct the badly developed skill, than to develop

it freshly. The nerve centres have been affected and the child naturally reacts in the way that have become habitual by practice and to change these nerve paths is very difficult.

In the case of learning, which is the assimilating of knowledge, we have a somewhat different process, which is as follows:

1. *Sensation*: Sensation is the awareness we have of objects in our environment through our senses. We see something, or hear something or smell it and so on. This is the way in which we describe sensations. So the first thing in learning, that is, in gaining knowledge, is sensation. This involves careful observation.

2. *Perception*: Following sensation comes perception which means interpreting sensation in the light of previous experience. A child sees a horse for the first time, and calls it a big dog. It has seen dogs before knows something about them, so interprets this new combination of sensations in the light of what it already knows. Thus, of course, is done quite unconsciously by the child.

3. *Association*: The knowledge gained through sensation and perception is then associates with what the child already knows and is made part of the child's mental stock. It becomes fixed in the memory and in the eye of the child. Relationships between different things are established.

4. *Generalization* (conception): This simply means the forming of general ideas and follows on from perception. Generalisation and association will often be going on at the same time.

5. *Use*: Finally comes the use of the knowledge gained. Generalizations are tested out in action and their truth established. Knowledge gained is expressed in action and thus made a real part of the make-up of the child. No knowledge is really part of us until we have used it. We cannot say we know a thing until we have put our knowledge into action in some way or other. Hence the importance of expression work in all learning which is assimilating of knowledge.

It will also be noted that the beginning of the process is of great importance. Accurate knowledge depends on accurate sensation. If we go wrong there then the whole process will go wrong. Hence, it is very important to train the senses of children.

Accurate observation not only with the eyes but with all the senses is essential to all accurate and satisfactory learning.

In this type of learning purpose also plays a great part. We deserve the things we are interested in those things which do not appeal to us, which have nothing to do with our purposes in life, we let go. Hence purpose will influence this whole process of learning. Not only will it motivate our learning, but it will determine what we learn and how we learn it. It is difficult to over-estimate the importance of pupose in the learning process of whatever type of learning we are thinking.

Factors Influencing Learning

There are various conditions of life and school which have a very definite effect on our pupils as they learn. If we wish to help them to learn and to make the most satisfactory adjustment to life, it is necessary for us to keep these conditions in mind. The following are the most important:

1. Learning depends on hereditary endowment.
2. Learning depends on the physical condition of children.
3. Learning depends on stimulation.
4. Learning depends on the goal set before pupils.
5. Learning is helped when pupils are given an active share in determining the goal and in planning how to reach it.
6. Learning is helped by associating things as parts of a total situation.
7. Fruitful learning depends on guidance and instruction.
8. Learning is affected by the emotional condition of pupils.
9. Learning is always the result of a total situation.

How to Improve Learning

Teachers needs certain tips or consideration to organize classroom learning which provide specific directions to the teacher. These considerations are helpful to the teacher to organize classroom teaching:

1. While deciding for learning of pupils, consideration for the capacities of the learner are very important.
2. Learning should be related to the developmental stages of the learner as suggested by Jean Piaget.

3. Learning varies from learner to learner due to individual difference.
4 A motivated learner acquires what he learns more readily than one who is not motivated.
5. Positive reinforcement or reward generally increases the pace of learning.
6. Learning with intrinsic motivation is much more useful and rewarding than learning under extrinsic motivation.
7. Learners need practice in learning to achieve excellence.
8. Active participation or involvement of a learner is useful than positive reception of knowledge.
9. Meaningful material and meaningful factors are learned more readily than superfluous material.
10. There is no substitute for repetitive practice in mastering the skills.
11. Timely feedback encourages the learner.
12. An effective teaching is always complementary to useful learning.

Instruction

Instruction is the process whereby students are inclined towards fulfilling the cognitive objectives of education. It is essentially one-sided, there is no interaction between the teacher and the student. Instruction is not the equivalent of education, although it can be included in or sub-sumed under the concept of education. The development of the cognitive aspect constitutes the limit of instruction whereas education is responsible for the development all of three aspects—cognitive, affective and psycho-motor—of the human personality. Thus, instruction is not education but a part of education, since it is limited to the child's intellectual aspect. Its objective is to complete the curriculum and to ensure that the child passes the test, instead of ensuring the child's development. In Instruction, the method of imparting information is artificial and compulsive instead of being spontaneous, with the result that only limited amounts of knowledge are absorbed by the child, and even those are retained generally quite temporarily. Hence, instruction cannot be equated with either narrow or liberal education, in fact, therefore, it can be seen as a part of schoolling the narrowest sense in which the term 'education' can possible be used.

	Education	*Instruction*
Objective	Maximum development of the child's various innate powers; transformation of his personality; His complete development.	Spread of information, facts and figures seeking the student's intellectual development.
Child's place	Central and most important.	Secondary; teacher and knowledge occupy the main place.
Child's Capacity	According to the child's ability, interest and attitude.	Complete neglect of these elements, imparting of information, facts and figures.
Knowledge	Stress on knowledge related to child's own experiences and real life.	Completely theoretical knowledge having almost no relationship between with real life.
Form	Formal and Informal, Comprehensive	Very narrow, nearly a part of formal education the knowledge imparted does not remain for long, *i.e.* temporary.
Performance	The knowledge imparted remains permanent.	
Method	Various methods	Spoon feeding through lecture; no place for mutual interaction.

(*Contd.*)

	Education	Instruction
Curriculum	The child's entire life is the curriculum, very comprehensive.	Very narrow, based on subjects and their systematic presentation.
Teacher	Various members of society, professionals.	Either professional instructors or machines and instructional programmes.
Evaluation	Both direct and indirect methods.	Not essential.

	Teaching	*Instruction*	*Learning*
1.	The aim of teaching is to impart knowledge, understanding or skill about a definite content.	Instruction is used for presenting certain facts before the pupils.	In learning certain experiences are provided to the pupil through teaching and the instruction.
2.	Teaching is a casual factor which may lead to certain behavioural changes.	Instruction is also a casual factor that may lead to certain behavioural changes.	Learning is a permanent change in behaviour.
3.	Teaching continues only in school.	Instruction continues only in school.	Learning is life-long process.
4.	Teaching is a broader than instruction but is limited to the content only.	Instrcution is narrow concept.	Learning is a broad concept.
5.	Teaching is formal.	Instruction is basically formal.	Learning is both formal and informal.
6.	Teaching is a social phenomenon.	Instruction is also a social phenomenon.	Learning is psychological phenomenon.

Training

The main purpose of training is to make an individual skilled in the performance of a specific activity. By performing particular activity repeatedly so many times, this kind of skill is obtained. Some scholars opine that training is skill based, and that while the mind is manifested more in learning, in training the main stress is upon the four limbs and their coordinated activity. According to Green, training can be employed in any activity in which mental activity is manifested in a lower proportion.

Training is neither education nor schooling, nor even instruction, but something distinct from all these. Training is an attempt to acquire or develop skill in this performance of a specific activity. What Rousseau calls the training of the limbs constitutes the first stage of training. However, teaching is not limited to the limbs, since even the sense organs of hearing, smell, vision etc., can be trained the four skills involved in the teaching of language—listening, speaking, reading and writing—are all obtained through training although they implicitly involve the training of the senses as well as that of the limbs. Hence, training comprehends both kinds of training.

Professional Education and Professional Training

Education is undoubtedly a very comprehensive concept, since it includes within its scope the entire range of human life. At present, a lot is being heard in the country about the 10+2 structure of formal education which consists of ten years of general educational to be followed by two years of professional education. From the viewpoint of entry into the professional or economic world, a tremendous emphasis is being placed upon the two years of professional education because it contains provisions for equipping the learner with many desired skills which can fit him for his entry into the competitive, professional world. In fact, it is an attempt at training for a particular profession. True professional education is that which provides for the training of individuals in skills required for a particular profession which places greater emphasis upon the practical aspect. Professional training is a very important component of professional education which makes an important contribution towards modifying the individual's behaviour with a view to specific profession. The comprehensive meaning of education often leads us to the use of the phrase professional education, whereas our actual intention is to speak of professional training. Seen thus, it is evident that training, too, is a part of education.

Difference between Education and Training

	Education	*Training*
Scope	Very comprehensive.	Very limited, at any one time, limited to only one activity; merely a part of education.
Aim	The all-round development of the child.	Development of one or more specific skills only.
Agencies	Formal as well as informal.	Training institutes, family etc.
Teacher	Members of formal and informal agencies.	Instructors.
Period	From birth to death.	A fixed short period (from a few days to a few years).
Place	Home, school, community neighbourhood etc.	Training institute, farm, factory.
Curriculum	Determined as well as indefinite.	Pre-determined, in conformity with the skill to be learnt.
Teaching methods	Varied.	Limited and fixed, changing only from one skill to another; main.
Evaluation	Direct/indirect given.	Direct.
Certificate	Given in formal education but not in informal education.	Given on the successful completion of training.

Memorization

In antiquity, the art of memorization was one of the fundamental arts related to the development of rhetoric. A speaker had to be able to remember the ideas he wanted to discuss and the order in which they were to be presented. A prerequisite for good oratory was a well-ordered mind, and part of the way of developing well-ordered mind was to memorize material in a systematic manner.

The Greeks and Romans distinguished two aspects of memory which they referred to as natural and artificial. Natural memory, was a memory for ongoing events. Artificial memory was memory for organised knowledge, the distinction has persisted until today. Later on the terms used as episodic and romantic memory, correspond rather closely to the distinction between natural and artificial memory of the ancients.

Most of the devices used by orators in Greece and Rome for memorizing the points to be covered in their speeches involved the use of imagery. A common recommendation was that one should begin memory training by learning to visualize the various parts of a familiar building in a systematic order. Thus one might learn to visualize the entrance, the foyer, and each nook and corner in the main chamber, in the order in which they might be encountered. When the points of a speech were to be memorized, the points then would be associated with the set of images of the parts of the building when the speech was given, the orator would imagine himself dwelling in each location where he would discuss the points associated with that particular location.

Perception and Memory

The meaningful perception of anything in the environment can occur only if the object of perception is related to what is stored in the nervous system. The prewired nervous system has built into it knowledge that makes meaningful perception possible from birth. Recorded knowledge provides the background against which experience is meaningful. Where an infant grasps an object and brings into the mouth, turning it and mouthing it the actions involved in doing this add to the information that can be derived from the object. The static holding of the object provides for less information about its properties than can be derived from turning the object and presenting it to the mouth in different positions. Later, the infant learns to hold objects before her eye and turn them in different positions for inspection there again, the action that the infant performs on the object increases the information that can be derived.

2

EDUCATIONAL OBJECTIVES

Teaching involves five essential processes; namely, defining goals or objectives, choosing content, deciding on methods of instruction, the instruction itself, and measuring results. To try to teach without defining objectives is like starting out on a journey without knowing where to go.

The good teacher formulates his objectives, chooses methods and materials in accordance with his objectives, employs these methods and materials, and uses measurement to determine how well or to what degree the objectives have been attained. In a sense everything is determined by the objectives.

Some teachers will not consciously formulate any Objectives at all, but will simply teach "by the book". Nevertheless, every teacher works towards some objectives, even if it is only to get through the text book by the end of the term. We are saying only that every teacher necessarily has some goals or objectives which give direction and purpose to his work.

The objectives or goals may be stated in different ways :

Robert Mager defined instructional objectives a "an intent communicated by the statement which describes a wanted change in learner." It laid emphasis on the changes to be installed in the repertoire of the learner after completion of the learning experience. In fact it gives the description of type of behaviour which the learner should be able to demonstrate after completing the leaning experience.

Dr. Paul Whitemore defined objectives as: "The statement of objectives of a training programme must denote measurable attributes observable in the graduation of the programme otherwise it will be impossible to determine whether the programme is meeting the objective or not."

In 1964 in a conference programmers reached the conclusion that the definition of an objective should be able to describe behaviour. It means that after the completion of a learning experience the student's behaviour like what he should be able to do or how he thinks or feels should be described.

Justification for specifying objectives

Question for the necessity of objectives has been debated by a lager number of educationists in different aspects. Some educationists gave their views in favour of it while some are against the specification of instructional objectives in behavioural terms. The general attitude of educationists is in favour of formulation of instructional objectives as they serve many-fold purposes. Some of which are as follows:

1. *Motivation*—To achieve the goal the leaner is always motivated by clearly defined objectives. By the help of objectives learner is able to arrange his efforts into relevant activities to reach the goal in advance. He does not have to learn irrelevant subject matter.

2. *Guidance*—Stratification of objectives in behavioural terms facilitate the teacher in selecting and organising the content. They serve as guidelines for evolving suitable teaching learning strategy for the teacher. The difficulties of students and teachers in interpreting are solved, all the ambiguity is removed and their task is limited by writing instructional objectives.

3. *Evaluation*—By the help of instruction objectives the evaluation of outcomes and performance of the learner can be made easily and it becomes possible to evaluate this in an objective way. Teacher can predict the success and failure of his way in which he presents the subject matter by evaluating the performance in terms of specified objectives. By framing objectives the measurement of learning experiences in a systematic and scientific way is ensured.

Characteristics of Good Instructional Objectives

Process of defining instructional objectives is as old as the process of defining instruction is. There is a great difference between traditional objectives and instructional objectives in behavioural terms. Traditional objectives are not developed by the teacher himself but are supplied to him by the Headmaster in the beginning of the session or are given in the book itself. They do not communicate with the intent of course in terms of behavioural terms.

Before comparing traditional objectives with instructional objectives in behavioural terms, let us see the characteristics of good instructional objectives.

A good instructional objective may be defined as the objective which can communicate with the reader, the programmer or the writer's instructional intent in definite and well planned language. The best way to describe the objective is to reach the goal by excluding the alternatives in the way. The definition of objectives should be such that the result or the outcome may be measured and observed in an objective manner. In order to sharpen his objectives the programmer, while formulating instructional objectives, must ask the following three questions. These questions are recommended by Robert Mager in his book "Preparing Instructional Objectives".

The first question : during demonstration of proficiency, what will the learner be doing. This question lightens the manifestation of actual behavioural operations by the help of which the learner will demonstrate the behavioural changes installed in his final repertoire after completing a learning experience.

The second question to be asked is related to the conditions under which specific behaviour will occur.

The third question is regarding the level of acceptable performance.

In addition to behaviour of learner the behavioural object should also specify the level of performance required by the learner. In order to frame up worthwhilc instructional objectives the programmes should always consider these questions.

Comparison between Traditional Objective and Behavioural Objective

Traditional Objectives	*Behavioural Objectives*
1. Traditional objectives do not have definite object. They	These are stated in definite terms with clear object.

do not communicate the intent of the teacher in definite terms.	They communicate the intent of the programme.
2. They are simply passed down on to the teachers by some dominating control authorities.	They are developed by the teacher or the programmer on their own.
3. They do not motivate the teacher and the student as these have no definite objective and are imposed by others.	To motivate the learner to achieve the decided goal by selecting and organising suitable method.
4. By this objective it becomes very difficult for the teacher to evaluate the performance and changes brought about in the learner's behaviour.	By this type it is very easy to observe and measure the behavioural change of the learner.
5. Traditional objectives are defined with trivial educational outcomes. Very frequently they reflect elementary mental processes.	These are defined in relation with many mental processes, ranging from simple knowledge to complicated problem solving.
6. They do not specify conditions for the occurrence of acceptable performance.	They specify the conditions for the occurrence of behavioural changes.

It has been found out that educationists who attempted first to develop programmes were sometimes confused in differentiating between goal and objectives. They sometimes used goal and the next time they used objectives whereas there are differences between goal and objectives. These are as follows:

Goal	*Objective*
1. It is a word with general sense of intent.	It has a definite sense or meaning.
2. It is an indefinite word without precision.	It is specific and prescribed word.

3. It does not help the teacher in deciding teaching strategy.	It is helpful to the teachers in deciding their teaching strategy.
4. It is not useful for directing the students.	It is useful for students in giving them direction with regard to the content and method of learning.

Considerations for Selection of Objectives

Present world is going through Sputnik age when knowledge is increasing at every second with a tremendous speed. This dilemma is like an explosion for learners like us who have to learn a lot to stand or make a separate place in this developing society around us, in a very little time. How shall we decide the worthy teaching objectives and what considerations shall we keep in our minds while selecting the objectives of a course or of a topic of the course. Ralph W. Tyler gave the following suggestions to the teachers and curriculum constructors to formulate worthful objectives. We in India can adapt the suggestions tendered by Tyler according to our socio-economic and cultural conditions:

1. With other things it is also equally important to teach the kinds of behaviour, those ways of feelings, acting and thinking that have an important place and value in our society and these help the learner in becoming an effective and impressive human being in the society.
2. Instructions should be planned in such a way that the initial stages of learning will remain under the supervision of the school. But continuous learning and reinforcement can and will take place outside the school, in home and society.
3. The third important consideration by Tyler is regarding the standard of the learner. Where does he stand in his educational development and what abilities does he bring to the given class? These informations should be properly planned.
4. The fourth consideration in selecting instructional objec-

tives is their relevance to the philosophy of education which is followed by a nation.

5. Fifth and the final factor important in selecting and stating instructional objectives is the consistency of these instructional objectives with the theory of learning.

By analysing the suggestions given by Tyler we find that these suggestions should be modified certainly before adapting them. These should be modified on the basis of our knowledge of educational philosophy and theory of learning. It is unfortunate that in India we have not yet developed the philosophy of education according to our requirements. We are simply following the mixture of philosophies and learning theories. Research is needed in this field of education.

Bloom's Taxonomy of Educational Objectives

Basically the idea to evolve a Taxonomy grew out of an attempt to resolve some of the confusions which resulted from the use of general terms as "to understand in different ways by different teachers and evaluators." With this objective in mind, the group of teachers from college and university under the leadership of Benjamin S. Bloom of Chicago University attempted to devise a framework or taxonomy that would hold meaning in place providing an inter-relating structure for different terms. Taxonomy of educational objectives is basicaliy a classification scheme; like the Binomial Nomenclature is the classification scheme for plants into family, sub-family, order, genus, species. In educational taxonomy the kind of behaviours, which we want to be displayed by the students as a result of learning process, are classified.

Educational taxonomy is an educational-logical-psychological classification system It makes educational distinction to sense that the limitations between categories reflect those decisions which the teachers make from the student's behaviours in the developments of syllabus in selecting the learning situations. It is a logical system in which the terms are precisely defined and are definitely used. Finally, the taxonomy seems to be definite with present understanding of psychological phenomenon.

The Taxonomy of Educational Objectives is quite advantageous.

First and foremost benefit is the analysis and classification of educational objectives in the cognitive, affective and psychomotor domains. With the help of taxonomy of educational objectives the teacher can state his educational objectives with greater ease and definiteness.

Secondly like the periodic table of elements, this taxonomy provides the panorama of educational objectives. The illustrative objectives may suggest ideas to be adapted in the areas being explored during the curriculum framing. For curriculum building the taxonomy has great importance with its hierarchical nature.

Major categories in the Cognitive Domain of Educational Objectives (Bloom, 1956):

1. *Knowledge*: Knowledge may be defined as the acquisition of factual information. Students have to learn specific facts, terms and methods which have a factual base. It is the lowest level of cognitive domain. In this recollection and recalling of information is required.

Assessment: The knowledge of students can be examined or evaluated by asking him direct questions or also by multiple choice test. Main objective of assessment is to test student's ability of recalling and identifying the facts and informations provided to him.

2. *Comprehension*: By the help of comprehension students shape their ability of understanding and presenting the material, idea, thoughts and theories. It is the lowest level of understanding the textual and graphic material or communication. It actually means the presentation of facts in a nice manner. The learner can abstract the theme out of the material and he can show his ability by presenting it in summary form.

Assessment: At comprehension level assessment needs more activity than the knowledge level. In this students can be asked objective questions as well as multiple choice questions but in a different order. Since they provide evidence that the pupils understand what they speak.

3. *Application*: It is related with the ability of students in utilising the principles or ideas in different consequence in which it was taught. In this case we want our students to be able to

demonstrate that they can apply their learned principles in different fields also at concrete situations.

Assessment: In case of application level the usual procedure of assessment by objective questions is totally altered. Here we create such situations where students can apply what they have learnt. For example, we give a child some fixed amount and ask him to buy the listed things from a general store. And then we make him calculate the amount spent and the money left with him. This example will prove his knowledge of addition and subtraction. But assessment of application becomes more complicated at advanced level of theoretical course.

4. *Analysis*: Analysis is a more advanced aspect than the previous levels. It refers to the student's ability of classifying or resolving the material into its components and understand the principle which organises this system or structure.

Assessment: The ability of analysing a thing can be assessed in many ways. We can ask the critical opinion of a student by giving him a problem. Objective of analysis involves the power of critical thinking by which we can separate fact from ideas and by comparing different theories we can give a fact based on logic.

5. *Synthesis*: At synthesis level the educational objectives refers to creativeness, the ability of framing a complete object by putting things together. This may involve the production of a unique communication. Synthesis emphasises on creating something new, making a new theory by putting different ideas together; which provide new insights and by the help of which students can create new ideas and enlighten the ones given to them by us.

Assessment: Assessment should be made in such a way so as to produce new ideas, methods and new principles. Programmer may use the criterion of writing stories, poems, painting or drawing any object or incident.

6. *Evaluation*: It is the highest level in the hierarchical development of intellectual abilities. In this case the results and outcomes of learning include elements of all the previous categories. It refers to the ability of judging the values of concepts, material and procedures, etc. for a specified purpose. We expect from our students to develop the ability of creating standard of judgement, to evaluate, to examine, to analyse and restrain the hasty judgment.

Assessment: We can judge the performances of students and others on the basis of standards accepted by the society.

Formulation of Specific Behavioural Objectives (Cognitive Domain)

For the formulation of statements of specific behavioural objectives in cognitive domain, a table provided with 3 columns is given on the next page. 1st column consists of taxonomic classification, in 2nd column appropriate infinitives which the teacher uses to achieve a precise wording for the desired behavioural change in the student and finally in the last column general terms related to the subject matter and its properties are stated.

The Affective Domain of Taxonomy

In communication between the affective domains dealing with attitude, interest and appreciation, there was great confusion. Suppose we say that after studying some theory related with art, the student is able to appreciate arts. What do we mean by this? Do we mean that he is aware of the usefulness of acts or he should go to the museum to learn about it himself? Do we mean that he should start regarding Arts due to its merits? Is he able to evaluate it and feel its effectiveness? All these questions suggest that all the three terms—attitude, interest and appreciation—are quite confusing and they create ambiguity in communication. In addition to these confusions the affective domain too presented some problems. For example the heirarchical domain was most difficult to be found out in the affective domain of the taxonomy. For the development of affective domain the principles of simple to complex and concrete to abstruct were not sufficient, something more was needed.

Krathuwohl, et al, 1964 attempted to discover a structure in the affective domain of taxonomy. They did research work and analysed the data. Analysis of affective objectives showed the following characteristics which are to be embodied by the continum:

1. The emotional quality is an important distinguishing feature of an affective response at certain level.
2. As one progresses up the continum it increases automatically.

Instrumentation of the Taxonomy of Educational Objectives: Cognitive Domain

S. No.	*Taxonomy Classification*	*Key Words: Examples of Infinitives*	*Examples of direct objects*
1.00.	Knowledge		
1.10.	Knowledge of specifics		
1.11.	Knowledge of terminology	To define, to distinguish, to acquire to identify, to recall, to recognise.	Vocabulary terms, terminology, meanings, definitions, elements, references.
1.12.	Knowledge of specific facts.	To recall, to recognise, to acquire, to identify.	Facts, factual informations, (sources, names, dates, events, persons, places, time periods), properties, examples, phenomenon.
1.20.	Knowledge of ways and means of dealing with specifics.		
1.21.	Knowledge of conventions	To recall, to identify, to recognise, to acquire.	Form(s), conventions, uses, usages, rules, ways, devices, symbols, representations, style(s), format(s).

1.22.	Knowledge of sequences.	To recall, to recognise, to acquire, to identify.	Action(s) processes, movements, continuity, development(s), trend(s) sequence(s) causes(s), relationship(s), forces, area(s), type(s), feature(s), class(es), set(s), division(s), arrangement(s), classification(s), category(ies).
1.23.	Knowledge of classification and categories.		
1.24.	Knowledge of criteria.	To recall, to recognise, to acquire to identify.	Criteria, bases, elements.
1.25.	Knowledge of methodology.	To recall, to recognise, to acquire, to identify.	Methods, techniques, approaches, uses, procedures, treatments.
1.30.	Knowledge of the universals and abstractions in a field.		
1.31.	Knowledge of principles, generalisations.	To recall, to recognise, to acquire, to identify.	Principle(s), generalisation(s), proposition(s), fundamental(s) law(s), principle element(s), implication(s).

(*Contd.*)

S. No.	*Taxonomy Classification*	*Key Words: Example of Infinitives*	*Examples of direct objects*
1.32.	Knowledge or theories and structures.	To recall, to recognise, to acquire, to identify.	Theories, bases, interrelations, structure(s), organisation(s), formulation(s)
2.00.	Comprehension.		
2.10.	Translation.	To translate, to transform, to explain to illustrate, to prepare, to read, to represent, to change. to rephrase, to restate.	Meaning(s), sample(s), definitions, abstractions, representations, words, phrases.
2.20.	Interpretation.	To interpret, to record, to rearrange, to differentiate, to distinguish, to make, to draw, to explain, to demonstrate.	Relevances, relationships, essential aspects, new views, qualifications, conclusions, methods, theories, abstractions.
2.30.	Extrapolation	To estimate, to infer, to conclude, to predict, to differentiate, to determine, to extend,	Consequences, implications, conclusions, factors, ramifications, meanings, corollaries,

		to interpretate, to extrapolate, to fill in, to draw.	effects, probabilities.
3.00.	Application	To apply, to generalise, to relate, to choose, to develop, to recognise, to use, to employ, to transfer, to restructure, to classify.	Principles, laws, conclusions, effects, methods, theories, abstractions, situations, generalisations, processes, procedures, phenomenons.

3. As one ascends the willingness to attend to the specified increases.
4. The developing integration of value pattern at the upper levels of continum.

Major Categories in the Affective Domain of the Taxonomy of Educational Objectives (Krathwohl, 1964)

Description of major categories of affective domain

1. *Receiving*: It means student's willingness to attend a particular phenomenon or stimulus. In this the classroom activities are included. From teaching point of view receiving is concerned with getting, holding and directing the student's attention. Learning results in this area range from simple awareness of a thing's existence to selective attention on learner's part. In affective domain "receiving" represents the lowest level of learning results.

2. *Responding*: It refers to the active participation of the student. At this stage student attends the particular phenomenon and reacts accordingly in some way or the other. In case of responding learning outcomes emphasise the following—

(i) acquiscence in responding—reads assigned material.
(ii) willing to respond—actively reads beyond assigned material.
(iii) satisfaction in responding—reads for self enjoyment.

In higher levels of responing there instructional objectives are included which are commonly classified under "Interest" *i.e.* which stresses upon the seeking out and enjoying particular activities.

3. *Valuing*: It is concerned with the value of a student who attaches to a particular object, phenomenon or behaviour. It ranges in degrees from simpler acceptance of a value (desires to improve skills in a group of students) to complexity of commitment (it assumes responsibility for the affective functioning of a group). Valuing is based on the internalisation of a set of specified values but hints to these values are expressed in the student's overt behaviour. Learning outcomes in valuing are concerned with constant and stable behaviour, which can make the values

clearly identifiable. In this category instructional objectives commonly classified under attitudes and application are included.

4. *Organisation*: Organisation is concerned with joining together different values, resolving conflicts between them and building of internally constant value system. Here the emphasis is laid upon comparison, relation and synthesis of values. Learning results with the conceptualisation of values (improvement of human relations by recognition of individual's responsibilities) or with organisation of a value system (development of a vocational plan which satisfies the necessity for economic security as well as social service). Instructional objectives relation to development of philosophy of life is included in this category.

5. *Characterisation by a value complex*: At this level of affective domain, there is a value system which controls his behaviour for a long time for him to develop into a characteristic life style. Thus the behaviour is perceivable, consistent and predictable. Under this learning outcomes include a broad range of activities but more emphasis is laid upon the fact; typical and characteristic behaviour of the student. Here the instructional objectives which are concerned with the student's general patterns of adjustment are appropriate (personal, social, emotional adjustments).

3. Major Categories in the Psychomotor Domain of the Taxonomy of Educational Objectives (Harrow-1972)

1. *Perception*: It refers to the learner's ability of becoming aware of his actions, objects, qualities or relations through his own senses and to make metals, physical and emotional preparatory adjustments (*e.g.* undergoes covert sensory behaviour).

2. *Imitation*: Imitation includes the learner's ability of performing an act according to instructions given to him but usually lacks any sustained control (*e.g.* performs actions which are impulsive and imperfect).

3. *Manipulation*: Manipulation means the learner is able to perform act according to given instructions rather than observation on pattern of imitation (*e.g.* performing and practising actions by following the given directions).

4. *Precision*: It means the ability of learner to practise and

perform different parts of a complicated task, by reproducing actions with control, accuracy and erectness).

5. *Articulation*: Articulation means the learner's ability of co-ordinating a series of facts by establishment of sequence and harmony (performances are with accuracy, control and speedy.)

6. *Naturalisation*: It refers to learner's ability of performing a thing automatically and spontaneously (*e.g.* performances become natural, routinised and smooth).

Other Taxonomies

Gerlach and Sullivan (1969) presented a taxonomy of educational objectives in cognitive domain which is altogether different from that of Bloom's taxonomy. They laid emphasis on the importance of over behaviour of learner. According to their opinion cognitive behaviour was classified into following 6 categories:

1. *Identify*: It involves the learner's ability to recognise whether a specific object or event is a member of the particular class or not.

2. *Name*: A referrant or a set of referrants is supplied with a correct name of it if not given before, by the learner.

3. *Describe*: It involves the learner's ability of reporting the necessary categories to object properties, events, even properties and/or relationship related with a designated referrant.

4. *Construct*: Here some productive work is done by the learner (*e.g.* drawing something, making an article of clothing or furniture whose specialisation is given to him either in class or in the test items itself.

5. *Order*: Arrangement of referrants in a correct sequence by the learner. The learner may be made to write the name or to give the full description of the referrant in a definite order.

6. *Demonstrate*: Learner performs the essential behavioural activities to the accomplishment of a designated object according to pre-established specifications

Gagne's Classifications

Regarding objectives of instruction Gagne made an extremely contribution. His classification is related directly to behaviour more than the Krathwohl and Bloom's taxonomies related to the

Exemples of General Instructional Objectives and Behavioural terms for the Psychomotor Domain of the Taxonomy

Taxonomy Categories	Illustrative General Instructional Objectives	Illustrative behavioural terms for stating specific learning outcomes.
Development of categories in this domain is still underway.	Writes smoothly and legibly; draws accurate reproduction of a picture (or map, biological specimen, etc.). Setting up laboratory equipments quickly and accurately, types with fast speed and accuracy. Performing dance steps correctly, demonstration of correct style of swimming, demonstration of skill in driving an automobile, repairing an electric motor quickly and effectively, creation of new steps in dancing, etc.	Assembles, builds, creates, changes celebrates, cleans, calibrates, composes, constructs, correction, creates, designs, dismantles, drills, fasters, fixes, follows, grinds, fixes, grips, heats, hooks, identifies, locates, makes, mends manipulates, mixes, paints, sends, sees, sharpens, sets up, starts, sketches, stirrs, uses, weighs, wraps, etc.

learning outcomes. Gagne's classificatian is related to the types of learning.

Robert Gagne who was one of America's premier instructional psychologists, has identified six types of objectives for description of intellectual skills to be produced in students. Each type of objective is related with a different kind of learning. Gagne's types of objectives are as follows:

1. *Reinstating*: Learner reinstates a motor or verbal stimulus. For example, recitation of a learnt poem or performing the basic actions involved in tieing a shoelace. This type is called chain learning.

2. *Discrimination*: Learner or the student is able to discriminate between two or more stimulating objects, which usually resemble with each other in some or the other respect. This type of learning is called discrimination learning which means to be able to discriminate or differentiate between two similar objects.

3. *Identification*: The student is able to identify an object by its quality like shape, size, colour by the appearance of the object. The type of learning involved in this case is called the "concrete concept learning".

4. *Classification*: In this category the learner or the student is to classify objects by defining them properly. The learning type is "Defined concept learning." Concepts like society and culture should not be denoted simply by pointing towards them but should be defined accurately. Classification makes the learner to use definitions rather than simply recalling informations of the past.

5. *Demonstration*: The learner can prove himself and his statements by demonstrating them. This kind is called the rule learning.

6. *Generation*: Last class of Gagne's taxonomy used generation in its verbal form "generate".

It is associated with "higher order rule learning". These rules are composed of two or more simpler rules. These cannot be simply applied or demonstrated but are found by the learner. The learner solves problems in enriched situations.

3

PREPARING THE PLANS

1. Yearly Plan

In yearly plan the teacher decides what the major ideas of dimensions will be dealt with during the year. For this yearly plan many things should be kept in mind, for example all the available text books, curriculum guides, course of studies and aids should be examined thoroughly. Joint preparation by all members of the department is the best method for the mating of the yearly plan.

Joint preparation helps in two ways:

1. Firstly promotes appropriate integration or combination of related courses and common method of teaching the same course.
2. Secondly, it leaves each instructor free to develop various aspects of the courses in one's own way.

It is unfortunate that some teachers rely only on one related textbooks for the yearly plan, this practice makes both teachers and students slaves to a single frame of reference. Textbook unit and topics are studied on a chapter by chapter basis. The textbook can merely provide learners with one comprehensive course of information. Since textbooks are designed to fulfil the needs of as many people as possible, they usually contain some materials of the marginal value to individual instructor. Since each textbook writer tends to emphasize certain aspects over others, the teacher should survey as many sources as possible in order to ascertain what aspects he or she will emphasize,

How are Major Course Concepts Identified

For instructional purpose identification of several broad ideas should be developed during the course and stated as declarative sentences. For example, from a course in general business, the course concepts could be:

1. Production standards in the United States make this nation the distribution centre of the world.
2. Retail markets in the United States are consumer-oriented.
3. Selling is a joint process of communication between buyer and seller.

After several tentative course concepts have been stated, they are revised and reworked until six or eight basic ideas remain. (Some teachers prefer to incorporate course concepts into course objects. This step is not essential, however.)

Frequently, two or more units may evolve from a single major concepts and thus create the need for more specific concepts. Eventually there will be a unit for each major points concept. Appropriate unit titles, based on the concepts give previously for a general business course, follow:

1. The United States: Distribution centre of the world.
2. The consumer determines the market.
3. Sales promotion and advertising.

After major unit titles have been tentatively established, an approximate time schedule reflecting the degree of emphasis to be given to each unit is established. Time limitations may necessitate basic changes. For example, sometimes certain units must be omitted (It usually takes three to six weeks to complete a unit).

How are major course purposes developed with students?

After selecting the major units the teacher provides the students with an overview of the major course aspects in order to give them an opportunity for developing expectation about the course, such an experience creates initial interest in the activities. This introduction takes the form of a lecture discussion.

Any instructional method or technique can be useful in attracting the students for the particular course of study. At least one class period should be devoted to this introduction.

Unit Planning

In the words of Nathan S. Washton, "Science teaching depends on the preparation of unified teaching lesson, blending the nature of the lesson, the personality and goals of the teacher, the climate of the class and the interests and the needs of the students with an appropriate selection of method."

This clearly indicate that good teaching includes the proper selection of content, formulation of objectives, organizing learning activities based on careful planning. The last factor namely careful planning is very important for the teacher, who is just entering in the profession of teaching, which will built confidence in him.

The present day teaching is very defective. Neither the teachers have developed the habit and interest to plan their lessons in advance nor the students are involved in this teaching-learning process. Unless there is deliberate planning for this by the teacher the teaching in the schools mainly is bound to suffer. Unit planning is one of the method for effective teaching.

What is a Unit

The concept of unit is the growth of psychology of learning which emphasises learning as a whole. A Gestalt approach includes the method of presentation and the matter to be presented.

A unit was considered to be a block of subject matter but the present concept of a unit includes the procedure of presentation of the subject matter that is both a block of content as well as method.

According to Preston: "A unit is a large block of related subject matter, as can be over-viewed by the learner."

Samford says that a unit is a "outline of carefully selected subject matter which has been isolated because of its relationship to pupils' needs and interests."

Unit Planning

The term 'unit' signifies the 'unity' or 'wholeness' for the learning activities related to some problems or topic 'planning' involves the selection of the proper, suitable paths from the alternative one therefore, 'unit planning' is the proper selection of learning activities which are closely related with each other and presenting a complete picture.

In other words, "the teaching unit, is neither a block of subject matter nor a series of independent lessons." For example in Physics heat, electricity, magnetism are a few examples of block of subject matter.

In Biology chordates, non-chordates, fungi are examples of block of subject matter. In Chemistry metallurgy, metals, non-metals are the examples of block of subject matter.

Unit planning gives us the guidelines for formulating the effective methods of teaching.

Types of Unit

According to James Michael Lee (Principles and Methods of Secondary Education, p. 275), there are two basic types of unit :

a. Resource unit.

b. Teaching unit.

(a) Resource unit is one which is intended to be a general guide in assisting the teacher to enrich the teaching unit. Thus the resource unit is for more general and comprehensive than the teaching unit since its aim is to raise the level of the teacher's knowledge of content and skill in pedagogy rather than the presentation of definite learning and their introduction into the actual classroom situation. Consequently, resource units will include such items as extensive bibliographies, suggested problems, areas, methods of analysing pupil needs and suggestions for evaluating various educational outcomes. Resource units are generally developed by a group of curricular experts and classroom teachers.

(b) *Teaching Unit* is one which is intended to be actually implemented by the teacher and the pupils in structuring a large related segments of a course. Hence it is considered to be most important type of unit for any teacher.

Basic Purpose and Functions of the Unit

1. The basic purpose of unit is to bring together various facts, ideals, values and attitudes into one cohesive form so that the pupil may understand actual reality of it.

2. A unit endeavours to develop a single grand generalization through the learning of associated facts, concepts and viewpoints.
3. The unit has the advantage of defining content and process limits and attempts to see one particular topic or problem at a time as related to full unit and to concentrate attention solely on this main area of study. This puts the unit on a sound cognitive and thomistic psychological basis.

Thus in Woodsuff's words (*Basic Concepts of Teaching*, p. 181) a unit is "guide to the formation of individual lessons."

Criteria of a Good Unit

While planning a teaching unit the following points should be considered:

1. It should include in view the needs, the capabilities and the interests of the pupils.
2. It should have a variety of field trips, experiments, demonstrations and projects etc.
3. It should take into account the previous experiences and background of the pupils.
4. It should provide new experiences which the students have not done before.
5. The length of this unit should be such as to maintain the interest of the students up to the last.
6. The material of the unit should consist of familiar and related topics and not of remote and strange ones.
7. It should be flexible so as to allow the above average pupils to go beyond the limits of the unit.
8. It should help, anticipate and satisfy some of the further needs of the pupils.
9. It should be related to the social and physical environments of the pupils.
10. It should be a part of a sequence that permits growth from year to year.
11. It should be the result of the joint planning of the teacher and pupil as far as possible.

Principles of the Planning

A systematic planning facilitates the teacher's work planning not only economises the time, efforts and resources but also contribute in attaining the preconceived objectives of the plan. A systematic planning is based on certain following principles.

1. *Plan should be Flexible*: Plan should be flexible as each student is different in his abilities, experiences, needs and interests. Each has its own attitude. Plan varies according to the school and community and the planning in school for today is not adequate for tomorrow. The important factor, in flexibi'ity, is the science teacher himself.

2. *Plan should be specific*: A plan should be specific as to how teacher learning process is expected to more forward and not vague. There should be specific provisions for the anticipated procedures, the content to be employed must be anticipated in more than a general way.

3. *Plan should be realistic*: The plan should be realistic and it should provide for wide ranges in ability and interest. The amount of time anticipated should be examined carefully. The teacher should assess his teaching carefully, and should find the adequate or additional resources or should plan in abundance because of a crippling deficiencies of the material apparatus, books and other teaching aids.

4. *Involving students in planning*: Students should be involved in the planning. This is an important step in planning. The references should be taken from some effective principles of teaching and learning and effective methods of science teaching etc.

Steps in Unit Planning

To examine a large number of actual units in written form, one should note that they vary substantially in organizational patterns and also to the extent to which the units are developed in detail. However, most of the units, in one form or the other includes following steps:

1. *Overview*: The purpose of overview is to describe the nature and scope of the unit and to introduce to the students with what they have to do from the begining to the end. Thus it enables the students to organize their learning experiences. This also helps the individual in motivation.

2. *Objectives*: It should include:

(a) **Basic Science Information:** It includes scientific facts, understanding, generalization, principles, laws, concept and conceptual schemes.

(b) **Desirable behavioural change**: It includes skills and both (mental and manual) scientific attitude, appreciation, interest etc.

3. *Learning situations*: It can be divided into 3 sub-headings:

(a) **Initiating activities:** It is the begining and introduction part of the lesson. It is to involve children in learning. It develops motivation curiosity and interest. This can be initiated by questioning, by raising problems by developing relation. With previous unit, by giving thought provoking experiments or demonstrations, by thought provoking discussion and by the use of film and film-strips.

(b) **Culminating activities**: The activities, which conclude the unit, are the culminating activities. Such activities encourage the students to organise learning in a pattern depending on all individual students.

(c) **Learning activities**: These are the means by which basic science informations are learnt and desirable changes in the child are developed. It is the middle and long part. Objectives are achieved by this part.

4. *Evaluation*: It is important part of the planning what students have learnt, must be evaluated. For judging the behavioural changes in child, proper methods of evaluation should be used.

5. *References*: At the end of the plan proper references should be given, so that children can be directed for further study relevant to the unit.

An analysis of above points reveals that a format of a good unit shows the answers of six simple questions:

1. Why? (Teacher objective)
2. Why? (Pupil objectives)
3. What? (Content).

Lesson Planning

Planning plays a very important role in the successful execution of any work. It is so in the case of teaching too. Planning will enable her/his to break-up the course into convenient units for each term, each month or each week. Thus she/he will not have to rush through the course towards the end of the session. In this way planning will have to do full justice to all the items in the syllabus ensuring their proper and systematic teaching, revision and consolidation.

Planning also enable the teacher to ensure that she does not over-emphasize one skill to the neglect of another. Some teachers lay too much stress on theoretical work and neglect practical work. If the teacher plans her/his lessons week after week she/he will be able to guard herself against his tendency of unbalanced development of various skills. In planning teacher is able to prepare her/his lesson thoroughly because she/he has to spend a good deal of time on their preparation. She/he thinks of ways and means of making her/his lessons interesting and lively.

What is a Lesson Plan?

A lesson plan may be defined as a "comprehensive chart" which outlines procedures to be followed to effect pupil learning within a prescribed time limit in a class. A lesson plan is also known as a 'blue print', 'a creative piece of work', 'a plan, or guide for action in the near future'. Lesson plan is arranged systematically in a logical sequence, to present learning experiences in the classroom. Lesson plan takes into consideration all the major variables that influenees it, for example the school set-up, intelligence and achievement of students, availability of teaching material and other physical facilities and the resourcefulness of the teacher.

A lesson plan may be long *i.e.* detailed one or quite short (brief). For a beginner in the art of teaching a detailed lesson plan is very helpful because he/she can anticipate all the difficulties or the problems who he/she will face during his teaching. After a long experience, it is possible for a teacher to prepare a brief outline which will reflect proper teaching-learning experiences.

Why We Plan Lessons?

There are many advantages of planning the lessons and

important ones are mentioned as follows:

1. The teacher can prepare his teaching plan in a systematic, logical sequence, which will help in proper learning to the students.
2. The teacher can anticipate all the difficulties or problems which he may face during his teaching.
3. The teacher can accumulate all teaching material which is needed for his good teaching.
4. A teacher can show his ideology which is related with new innovations in education and can practice it in the classroom.
5. A lesson plan helps in the preparation of first class instruction.
6. A lesson plan develops self confidence, security in the individual teacher.

Important Elements for Lesson Plans

A lesson plan requires the following elements:

1. The teacher should have the mastery of subject matter.
2. He should have the ability to content analysis and identifying learning objectives in terms of taxonomic categories.
3. He should have the ability and skill for writing objectives in behavioural term.
4. He should have ability to select the appropriate teaching aids in view of the content and objectives to be achieved.
5. The teacher must have the competency in relating teaching activities to learning structure by using appropriate teaching and communication strategies.
6. He should be able in constructing criterion test for evaluating the students learning outcomes.
7. He should be able in planning, organizing reinforcing the students activities, and controlling their behaviours.
8. He should have the knowledge and skill for working questions for developing the lesson plan.
9 He should have the skill for the effective use of blackboard in presenting the content.

10. He should have the awareness of individual differences of the students and should make the provisions in lesson plan to adjust the individual differences.

Bases of Lesson Planning

An effective plan helps the teacher to promote maximum learning. A teacher can prepare a lesson if he understands its mechanism which is based on certain theoretical assumptions. Just to understand there assumptions, J.K. Sood (1986) has divided them into three parts which are as follows:

1. Preliminary knowledge and abilities needed for lesson planning.
2. Steps or essentials to be considered in lesson planning.
3. Evaluation of a lesson plan.

1. *Preliminary Knowledge and Abilities*

Preliminary knowledge and abilities needed for lesson planning should be based on the following:

1. Writing specific objectives and selection of concepts.
2. Selecting and organizing learning experiences.
3. Selecting methods or strategies which you will use.
4. Identifying the materials and Audio-Visual aids needed for the specific lesson.
5. Set induction. As a teacher how will you introduce your lesson?
6. How will you find out that you have achieved the set objectives?
7. Closure: The closure brings a lesson to an end.

(ii) *Steps in Lesson Planning*

Steps to be considered in a lesson plan may differ from teacher to teacher. But some of these are needed in a systematic lesson plan. These are as follows:

1. General information about the class, students, subject, time, etc.
2. Writing of specific objectives.
3. Instruction aids needed.
4. Previous knowledge of the students.

5. Method or methods to be used.
6. Introduction of the lesson or set induction.
7. Development of the lesson.
8. The closure which includes recapitulation also.
9. Black-board summary.
10. Home assignments,
11. References.

(iii) *Evaluation of a Lesson Plan*

Evaluation of a lesson plan depends on many factors because alongwith educational and technical considerations, it involves personality and philosophy of the teacher. However, some considerations can be as follows:

1. Are the specific objectives clear ?
2. Is the lesson plan rich in content ?
3. Is it rich in learning activities ?
4. Is it sufficient about materials used ?
5. Is it effective on introduction (set induction) development, and recapitulation (closure) ?

Factors Affecting Lesson Planning

There is no guarantee that a lesson plan developed by a teacher for his/her use, will be a success at every time. It is because many factors influepce lesson planning and the success of its presentation depends on them. These factors are given by J.K. Sood as fol'ows:

1. The school: urban or rural.
2. The number of children in the class.
3. Average age of students.
4. Their standard of attainment.
5. Children's knowledge assumed by the teacher.
6. Aims of the lesson.
7. Availability of teaching aids.
8. Personality and philosophy of the teacher.

Therefore, all these factors should be taken into consideration while planning a lesson

Parts of a Lesson Plan

It is a general practice to write detailed notes on units and lesson plans in steps or stages. With the passage of time, these steps or stages have acquired a natural status. These steps do not clarify any psychological principles except that they appear to be based on common sense. For example, these (logical) steps do not inform the practicing teachers about the princlples of learning or the basic concepts in learning namely: conditioning, reinforcement, creativity in thought, accommodation and assimilation, and the acceleration of mental development etc.

In the light of the above, it is possible to arrive at the following parts of a unit and a lesson plan. The parts shade into each other. These parts need not follow in the sequence given this sequence will naturally depend upon the objectives to be achived, the type of activities to be initiated, the physical facilities available, the mentality of students and also their number in the class.

1. Basic Information.

   (a) Subject
   (b) Title of the Unit
   (c) Tilte of the Lesson
   (d) Class
   (e) Date
   (f) Total number of periods.
   (g) Time estimates.

2. Statement of Objectives

These should be in terms of pupil behaviour and functional understanding:

   (a) General
   (b) Specific

3. Instructional and illustrative material to be used.
4. Pre-text situations to test the previous knowledge.
5. Proceducre/approach to introduce the unit/lesson.
6. Introduction to the unit/lesson:

   (a) General
   (b) Specific

7. Recapitualation.
(at the end of the unit/lesson).
8. Application.
9. Summary of the unit/lesson.
10. Evaluation.
11. Assignment.
12. References for self and students.
13. Self evaluation.

The above parts of a lesson will vary from lesson to lesson, because it is governed by the content and method used in the particular lesson. Many times the availability of instructional material and other physical facilities also influence all these parts of a lesson.

There is no hard and fast rule of using these parts, yet these help in preparing a proper sequential plan for teaching. It will be more useful for a teacher if he assesses a few self searching questions prior to planning a lesson. For example:

1. Why am I teaching this lesson? What are my aims and objectives of this lesson ?
2. Are these aims stated in terms of pupil's behaviour ? Can they be achieved at the end of the lesson or the unit ? Are these aims suitable for the class, I am going to teach?
3. Have I chosen learning experiences (relevant, significant and meaningful, worthwhile) cansistent with the specific aims and objectives of the lesson?
4. Is it possible to demonstrate all the experiments? Is it possible to take help from the students and the conduct of certain experiments ? Do I need any illustrative material for this lesson from the community or any other external agencies? Are these materials suitable for all the pupils?
5. Can I approach this lesson in some other ways ? How much background knowledge do the students possess about the topic, I am going to teach?
6. Can I relate this lesson to daily life?
7. Do I think the students will be well motivated throughout the lesson?

8. Have I considered individual differences among my students?
9. How am I meeting them in my lesson? Can I finish this lesson in time?
10. How will I summarize the main ideas of this lesson? Can I help students to develop black-board summary with some help?
11. What home work should I set to my students?
12. How can I evaluate this lesson? Has quality been built into test items and questions I am going to ask them in the class?
13. How does this lesson fit in with lessons already taught and likely to be taught?

After studying these questions, it shall be possible to prepare a lesson plan. The proformas used in lesson plans differ from institution to institution, and from teacher to teacher. One example of proforma is given below:

Class:	Subject:	Time estimated
Period:	Topic:	Age Level:
		Date:

1. Objectives:
   (a) General
   (b) Specific
2. Teaching Aids.
3. Procedure.
4. Previous Knowledge.
5. Introduction.
6. Development.

Teacher's Activity	Students' Activities

7. Recapitulation.
8. Black Board summary.
9. Home Assignments.
10. References.
11. Self evaluation.

Characteristics of a Good Lesson Plan

A good lesson plan is written, characterised by the following. It has :

1. Clear statement of all the steps and the objetives to be achieved.
2. Allocation of time to each phase of the lesson.
3. Orderliness and flexibility.
4. Continuity of the old and new subject matter with upto-date information.
5. Appropriate motivation and evaluation techniques.
6. Illustrations and pivotal questions.
7. A variety of teaching and learning procedures.
8. Provision for individual differences.
9. Scope for extensive use of problem-solving as the basic developmental procedure.
10. Good summary and assignment.

Some common faults to be avoided in the lesson plan are:

1. Over-completeness or too many details or rigidity of the plan;
2. Disconnectednes;
3. Using the same techniques throughout; and
4. Too much dependence on book.

Assignment

This method is the combination of the lecture demonstration method and the individual laboratory work done by the student. It includes the merits of both the methods and is a good method of instruction for the students of Higher Secondary classes. The assignment should be, well planned according to the age, interest and aptitute of the veriety of students.

The whole year's work is divided into number of well connected portion which should be covered in a week or the so called assignments. Pupils are asked to do this assignment according to their will. The only thing is that it should be finished in time. For the assignment the students are required to go through their lessons from the books related to the assignment. By the assignment the pupil prepare a part of theory and a part of practical work.

An individual record of every pupil is maintained by the teacher which serves as a sort of stimulant on the part of pupil. Thus assignment serves as a key for testing the abillty of the pupil. Assignment prevents the pre-examination cramming and different literature. There are two types of assignment prevalent in the high schools.

Home assignment : In this system pupils are asked to write answers to the questions assigned by the teacher. References of the different sources concerning the topic are given by the teacher. The pupils group the ideas of the text books, journals and other available sources for the concerning there assignment. Pupils answer of the questions eoncerning their assignment and bring them to school. The teacher goes through their work and finds out the discrepacies. If she thanks that the answer of their questions is not appropriate, she asks them to refer after books concerning the topic. With the help of the instruction given by teacher pupils proceed on their work.

School Assignment: In this system pupils perform experiments related to their work and answer the questions asked by the teacher. Generally, one third of the periods in the week are reserved for demonstrations given by the teacher and one third for the individual laboratory work. The teacher demonstrates the difficult experiments which require the specific technique. The easy and simple practicals are assigned to the students. For guidance a sheet of information is given to the students before performing the experiments. They go through the instruction and answer the quertions asked, in their note books. This is then handed over to their teacher one day before their practical work whose home assignment is completely satisfactory. The teacher maintains the record of the work with her for each pupil. This record helps the teacher which pupil is strong and who is weak. According to this she gives the instruction to the pupils.

Objectives of assignment: Assignment method should attempt to achieve the objectives for which the subject is taught. It should provide training in particular subject. By introducing new and wider avenues of the subject interest among the students should be developed. It should help the student to discover new facts and wider concept of that subject so that they may be able to apply them into appropriate forms and principles.

Criteria of Good Assignment

While framing an assignment the following points are to be kept in view. They are:

1. The question-answer should be related to the topic under discussion. An isolated assignment never becomes satisfactory.

2. The assignment should be brief but complete, so that the students will be able to comprehend his implications.

3. It should be clear in its purpose and should aim at realising the necessary objectives. Instead of teaching only theoretical knowledge assignment should test various aspects such as comprehension application, techniques, skills, interests, and attitude of pupils.

4. The presentation of questions should be such that it should stimulate the reflective thinking and should give freedom to the students to discover the things themselves.

5. Teaching becomes quite effective if the assignment is set according to the suitability of age, intelligence, interest and ability of the student. If possible different assignment should be given more preference in selecting the assignment herself/himself that intervens her/him about the topic he is quite confident. In case of the group assignment the brighter students may select difficult part while the weaker ones may select the easier parts. As a result of this students according to their abilities will progress satisfactorily in learning process and the rate of work will suffer.

6. It should create curiosity among the pupils and should be sufficiently thought provoking and challenging. A mountain assignment should not be given. It will not arose any interest in the pupils, rather will create monotony.

7. It should not be rigid and binding. As the students are interested in solving the problems arising from a situation and therefore the teacher should make it a point to assign those related problems to the student. For example if the student is

interested in making chart the teacher should assign him the work of making chart.

Planning and assignments

The success of this method is mainly dependent on the assignment drawn out by the teacher. When an assignment is given:

1. An advance preparation should be made at the beginning of the unit.

2. Various problems come during the learning of the unit. For all these occasions the teacher should keep in view the following points while preparing assignment.

(i) The teacher should divide the syllabus into as many assignments as they are permissible under the time at her disposal. This work can be done by counting the working days of the year with the help of calender.

(ii) The learning process involved in the teaching of unit should be analysed by the teacher. The objectives of her plan should be set down and same objectives can be realised by a number of assignments but the teacher should select that which suits the best.

(iii) In order to fulfil the aim of the assignment it should be planned keeping in view the age, intelligence, interest, abilities etc. of the pupils. Assignment should be planned with the cooperations of the pupils concerned.

(iv) It should be based on good text books. The teacher should see that the referred text books are within the comprehension of the students. Reference pages should be indicated against each question. The important facts or principle should be earmarked by the teacher which will certainly draw attention of the pupil. This will help the students.

Thus the teacher can maintain the enthusiasm and interest of the students. Teacher should also allot time for the various facts of an assignment.

(v) The assignment questions should be in the clear, exact and easily in understandable language. The teacher should also keep a set of questions to evaluate the achievement of the assignment by the pupil.

(vi) The teacher should give a detailed information related to the materials used for the practical work, precautions and method to be adopted for the practical work. What technique the pupil should follow in the observation and results of the practical work the instruction for all should be given on the instruction sheet.

(vii) For practical work the assignment questions should reduce the method of procedure, recording, calculating and setting up the material.

Merits of Assignment

1. This method is based upon the principle of "learning by doing" which provides full opportunity to the students to work in the laboratory. They learn to handle the apparatus, develop team spirit and their curiosity, acquisition and instincts find satisfaction.

2. The teachers can pay attention towards the individual student. She can motivate and guide the students without interfering in the work of the students. This develops the relationship between them.

3. This method provides individual opportunity in the learning process. Each student works at his/her own rate and no one stands in the way of the other. Even the absence of a student from the school for a day or two does not harm him/her much, as by the lecture method. She/he can carry on with the preparation part of the assignment even at home or start his/her assignment when he/she comes back to the school.

4. The students form the habit of self-study. They receive necessary training in extra study, removing the doubts by consulting the dictionary, charts, maps and other reference books and gather the desired data. In this way, attitude of self reliance, self dependence and self expression are developed among the students. Extra study widens their outlook and sphere of the knowledge.

5. The different assignments depend upon their progress and interest.

6. This method is based on scientific principles and procedures. It helps in developing the scientific attitude and in the training in the scientific method.

7. As the teacher gathers an idea from the "progress chart" about the weaker and brighter students. She/he can check the weaker and the specinker student and give instruction to him for improvement.

Failure of the assignment is based on the following reasons:

1. Lack of good standard of literacy.
2. Due to the language difficulties and non-availability of good text books.
3. Requirement of the reading rooms.
4. Assignments are based on a single text books.
5. Pupils may not actually be doing work; they might have copied it from others. This can be checked by asking questions at the time of the practical work.
6. Practicals are isolated from the theory work.
7. This is a slow procedure and it will be difficult to finish the heavy curriculum in the limited time.

This method is quite suitable for the higher classes because the students acquire sufficient knowledge to understand the common principles relating to the particular subjects. The success of this method solely depends upon a well-planned assignment by the teacher. Besides all other limitations no student should be allowed to proceed further unless and until he has finished his first assignment.

4

TEACHING SKILLS

Introduction

Let us examine the term teaching before we pass on to teaching skills. In the complex act of teaching, one complex organism (teacher) directs towards more complex organism (students) in the complex situation (classroom) to cause one of the most important activities called "teaching". Complexity of the activity of teaching is evident from the fact that nobody exactly knows "What teaching is ?" Ban has exactly remarked that teaching means many different things, that the teaching act varies from person to person and from situation to situation. This is the reason for so many definitions of teaching.

Gage tentatively defines, "teaching" as an act of inter-personal influence aimed at changing the ways in which other persons can or will behave. According to Ryans "the behaviour or activities of persons they go about doing whatever is required of teachers, particularly those activities which are concerned with the guidance or direction of the learning of others." According to Skinner, "teaching is the arrangement of contingencies of reinforcement under which students learn. They learn without teaching in their natural environments, but teachers arrange special contingencies which expedite learning, hastening the appearance of behaviour which would otherwise be required slowly or making scene of the appearance of behaviour which might otherwise never occur."

From these definitions it can be concluded that teaching is an activity like (a) imparting knowledge or skill, (b) it is a social act of influence, and (c) it is doing anything and everything that may lead to learning.

With a view to reducing the complexities of the process, Gage has suggested 'micro-criteria' approach to teacher effectiveness. In the effort, he pointed out that, "rather than seeking criteria of effectiveness of teachers in making varied facts of their role, we may have better success with criteria of effectiveness in small specially defined aspects of roles. Many specific problems have been solved by being analysed into smaller problems whose variables are less complex". Teaching is analysed into a number of teaching acts/behaviours when micro-criterion is applied in teaching. For example during his classroom activities, the teacher is engaged in a number of activities, most of which are done by him with one aim to promote learning among his pupils. All these teaching activities which include introducing a lesson, demonstrating, reinforcing, providing feed-back, explaining, illustrating, questioning, writing on blackboard, drawing figures etc. These verbal and non-verbal activities are called teaching activities. Hence, specific teaching acts/behaviours which are measurable, observable, demonstrable and can be developed through training, are known as teaching skills. In other words, a teaching skill is defined as a set of teacher behaviours which are especially effective in bringing about desired changes in pupils. Teacher uses these skills in pre-instructional, instructional and post-instructional stages in order to achieve pre-decided objectives.

DISCUSSION

In discussion ideas of many pupils are gathered through discussion. Both class and group discussions can be made use of by an encouraging and sympathetic teacher. This method can be used either exclusively or in combination with other methods. Its advantages can be listed as follows :

1. It is useful to know more of the pupil's background.
2. It is helpful for promoting better participation of pupils.
3. It is appropriate to make the class more lively, active and interesting.
4. It develops leadership qualities and responsibilities.

Discussions are useful to stimulate group thinking in a class. During discussion pupils learn to state their viewpoints and express their ideas frankly. Discussions are more effective than a lecture in classifying thinking, They promote pupil participation.

There is an interchange of questions and ideas among the participants. This method contributes to the application of the materials learned, and to building attitudes that are important in shaping behaviour patterns.

Effectiveness of discussion depends on several factors :

(i) Age level and abilities of the students.
(ii) Class size.
(iii) Subject matter.
(iv) Experience and skill of the teacher.

The teacher must thoroughly prepare for the discussion. Pupils think together effectively only when conditions are favourable. The pupil need :

(i) a sense of belonging;
(ii) a share in planning the goals;
(iii) a feeling of contributing to human welfare of group endeavour;
(iv) definite signs of progress towards the goals set;
(v) a feeling of confidence.

The aids should be properly used. The blackboard is a great help to clear thinking and helps the pupils to keep the points of discussion in view. All discussions should be closed with accurate summaries.

The discussion methods play an important role in the development of social behaviour and prepare for citizenship in a democratic society.

Learnings resulting from discussion

(i) Getting acquainted with other people.
(ii) Learning ways of working with others.
(iii) Developing respect for others' ideas and feelings.
(iv) Learning to put the interest of the group above self.
(v) Developing a sense of commitment for accomplishing the work of the group.

(vi) Realising that the product of group effort is superior to the best efforts of any single member.

Role of the teacher :

(i) Introducing the subject.
(ii) Allowing time for the group to warm up and keeping the discussion from deviation.
(iii) Maintaining the spirit of the members high by encouraging informality, ease of conversation and humour.
(iv) Orienting the students to the discussion technique and to the particular topic to be discussed.
(v) Creating the proper climate for free interchange of ideas.

The points to be discussed should be listed cooperatively with the students. Materials to provide background information should be made available.

A final summary should highlight the conclusions reached. At times stage, generalisations applicable to other situations can be formulated.

The teacher at the end may emphasise important ideas, correct mistakes of the students and suggest possible class activities as outgrowths of the discussion.

Student participation

Shy students should be encouraged and helped to take part in discussion. A well-informed student with leadership quality may also guide the group. Each student should feel the importance of his contribution to the discussion. Facilities should be provided for prior preparation so that after discussion a pool of ideas will make the discussion productive and fruitful. All will have equal right to contribute, there should be an atmosphere of friendly cooperation among the students. They should learn to respect honest differences of opinion.

Variations of discussion method

(i) Panel discussion.
(ii) Discussion 66.
(iii) Buzz session
(iv) Brain-storming.

(v) Symposium.
(vi) Debate.

(i) Panel Discussion : It is a discussion among a group of 4 to 10 persons on a subject. They present views before an audience which joins in the discussion subsequently, only informal conversation takes place. The participants talk on different aspects of a problem. The purpose is to :

(a) get important facts from different angles;
(b) stimulate thinking;
(c) to lay a basis for wide participation.

The chairman introduces the members to the audience and states the problem. The members give their views. Each speaks for a few minutes. Then free discussion follows between the members and the audience. The chairman summarises the panel discussion and brings out the important points emphasised. Panel discussion is dealt with separately in this book in detail.

(ii) Discussion 66 : The name arises from the fact that 6 persons meet for 6 minutes to discuss a problem (each member for one minute). The method is useful when it is necessary to get the opinion of a majority of the pupils in a minimum time.

(iii) Buzz Session : The class breaks of into pairs to discuss on issue and changes partners at the buzz (ringing) of a bell. At the end, each records the suggestions heard.

(iv) Brain-Storming : The brains of the participants are stimulated to create a storm of ideas and suggestions regarding a topic. Any idea whatsoever, is accepted. But unless there is person-to-person informal relationship between the teacher and the pupils and amongst the pupils themselves, they cannot speak freely.

This technique is usually used by business firms to encourage creative ideas. The storm of ideas help in solving a problem.

A simple particular problem familiar to students and having a number of solutions is selected. Students differ their own ideas and at the same time give suggestions how to improve the ideas of others, to produce a combination of ideas for solution of the problem.

The teacher announces the problem earlier to enable the

students to prepare in advance and then come for discussion. The teacher must have creativity so that the final solution is a novel one. Follow-up of the solution may be taken up to test its reality.

(*v*) *Symposium* : Each member of the group gives his views on a particular aspect of the problem as a specialist. At the end, there is a mutual discussion or question-answer.

(*vi*) *Debate* : Debate is organised between two groups. One group offers arguments in favour of and another group against a particular topic. Members of each group try to answer the arguments of the opponents. In formal debates judges are there to judge the superiority of a group.

DEMONSTRATIONS

Demonstrations are used to provide information to create interest or to develop standards of work by sharing how certain things are done. Demonstrations can be short and informal. Demonstrations can be given by one or more pupils or by the teacher alone or by the teacher and the pupils working together. For a good demonstration, different steps should be planned, demonstrated and then reviewed.

The factors characterising good demonstrations are : (a) preparatory period when its need and purpose are classified, (b) the demonstration itself, and (c) follow up period to practise the process or skills demonstrated. Characteristics of good demonstrations :

1. It will show the steps in the process accurately, clearly, definitely and in consecutive order. They must be listed on the blackboard.
2. The teacher talks and asks questions while working.
3. The procedures shown and the materials, equipment and articles and the processes used should be similar in size and bind to those the pupils use.
4. Only one process should be demonstrated at one time. Until the fundamental process is thoroughly understood, it is not advisable to introduce variation.
5. Equipment and materials required must be carefully selected and kept ready within reach.
6. Opportunity must be given during demonstration for question from the pupils.

7. Additional suggestions should be given for practice and use of the one process demonstrated.
8. Steps in the process demonstrated should be summarised at the end, preferably by the pupils themselves.
9. The article made during the demonstration should be left on the table or bulletin board for inspection, if possible. It will help to refresh the steps.
10. Help of visual aids must be taken to enhance understanding.
11. Demonstration should be followed by practice under close supervision. If manipulative skill is the goal repetition of the practice in the class and home experiences will be needed to bring the ability to the desired level.
12. Evidences of the success of the demonstration are : (a) interest of pupils in voluntary and continuous, (b) follow-up work is successful with little supervision from the teacher, (c) only few pupils need individual help during subsequent practice.

In the demonstration method both lecture room and laboratory work are taken into account. In a school, the lecture room is a place for teaching and the demonstration table is the teacher's laboratory table. The assembled students listen, observe and make notes. In this method the teacher works and experiments with the help of the students. The lesson consists of questions and answers. All the questions are direct and of leading type. There are mainly two reasons for using of the above method :

1. It becomes easy to do practice after demonstration.
2. Practicals are less expensive than pupils individually conducting practicals. It also saves time.

EXPLAINING

In the classroom teacher uses a number of interrelated statements related to the concepts, phenomena, generalisations and function with a view to developing in pupils an understanding about them. The set of interrelated statements used for this purpose is termed as explanation and the process is termed as explaining. The term explaining can, therefore, be defined as the use of inter-related statements about a concept, phenomenon or generalisation with a view to providing its understanding to some one else. Whenever the teacher explains anything, he should keep previous knowledge of the pupils in his mind. The quality of an explanation, however, depends on the degree of understanding it generates in the students.

Types of Explanation

There are mainly three types of explanation—the descriptive, the interpretative and the reason giving. They approximate to the questions 'How ?', 'What ?' and 'Why ?'. A descriptive explanation describes the process structure or procedure of phenomenon, generalisation or principle. For instance the concept such as 'How is the Nitrogen gas prepared' ? requires descriptive explanation on the part of the teacher. An interpretative explanation specifies the central meaning of the concept, generalisation or the phenomenon. For example what is electricity ? A reason giving explanation specifies reasons for the occurrence of a phenomenon, events, or the basis of a principle. For instance when a teacher is to explain as to why we use the nitrogen gas in electric bulbs, his explanation would be termed as reason giving explanation. In the explanation of a particular concept, all the three types of explanation will be needed.

The effective explanation involves increase in the occurrence of desirable behaviour and avoidance of undesirable behaviour.

Desirable Behaviour

The following desirable behaviours are required for effective explanation :

1. Use of appropriate beginning and concluding statements.
2. Use of explaining links like 'such as', 'due to', 'in spite of', 'as a result of', 'therefore', 'because', 'in order to', 'the main purpose'.
3. Covering of essential points.

1. *Undesirable Behaviour* : The following undesirable behaviour hinders the effectiveness of explanation. It is essential for the teacher to avoid the use of irrelevant statements because statements unrelated to the concept hinders pupil understanding and sometimes confuses the pupils.

2. *Lacking fluency* : Uncalled for interruptions in the flow of an explanation due to fumbling ideas and inapprapriate words or statements, hinder pupils' understanding of the concept. Obviously smooth and uninterrupted flow of statements makes the explanation clear and effective.

3. *Lacking continuity in statements* : As an explanation is a set of interrelated statements concerning a concept or a generalisation, the interrelatedness between the sentences is on the basis of logical sequence. The missing link between statements in a sequence causes break in the continuity for an explanation. Lack of continuity in the explanation, thus makes it difficult for the pupils to understand the concept or generalisation.

4. *Using inappropriate vocabulary* : An explanation to be understood by pupils should contain vocabulary appropriate to their age, grade and maturity level. Use of vocabulary not known to pupils hinders their understanding of the phenomenon. Further, the use of certain vague words and phrases such as probably, perhaps, in fact, actually, etc. makes an explanation vague. A teacher should avoid the use of such words which make an explanation vague and hinders its understanding.

ILLUSTRATING WITH EXAMPLES

Many times it happens that a teacher explains in the classroom a scientific principle, or a mathematical rule or an abstract idea and observes that his pupils are not comprehending it. In such a situation, the teacher attempts to explain the concept or generalisation more and more but he fails in his attempt. The concept or generalisation requires more and more explanation for the pupils to understand. This presents a challenge to the teacher. An unskilled teacher may deal with this challenging situation by rebuking the pupils for being inattentive in the classroom and asking them just to memorise the concept or rule. But a skilful teacher handles this situation in a different way. He illustrates the scientific principle, generalisation, the abstract idea concept or mathematical rule with the help of examples. This makes them easier to understand for the pupils. Obviously, examples are one of the most effective tools in the hands of the teacher to make the concept or generalisation simple and easier for pupils to understand. Thus examples can be defined as "the observation or situations of occurrence of a concept or generalisation" and the skill of illustrating with examples can be defined as the selection and presentation of the examples, relevant to the concept or generalisation to be taught to the pupils so as to make it easier for them to understand it." The examples, of course, may be drawn from the pupils experiences.

The next logical question is as to whether all examples make the concept or generalisation easier to understand. If not, what type of examples are helpful and appropriate in realising this objective ?

1. **Formulating simple examples**

Simple examples provide help to students in understanding the concept or the generalisation. The word simple is relative term and it does not have absolute meaning. An example which is simple for IX grade pupils may not be simple for VI grade pupils. Similarly, an example which is simple for pupils of city schools may not be simple for pupils of rural schools. Further an example which is simple for a particular grade of pupils in one country may not be simple for the same grade of pupils in an another country because of the cultural differences. Simple examples, therefore, are the one which are based on the previous experiences of the pupils. They gain experiences through a variety of sources like studying books, meeting people, interacting with peers, teachers and media, visiting places etc.

Simple Example

Q. What happens to iron rod when it is heated from one end ?

A. It gets hot and red.

Q. What happens to the hot rod when it is allowed to cool?

A. It changes into its original position.

Q. What happens to boiling water when pan is covered ?

A. It is converted into vapour.

Q. What happens to the covered pan containing vapours is cooled ?

A. Vapours changes into water.

Teacher statement—In these examples, we see that there is a change in some of the physical properties such as colour, shape and the state of matter, but there is no change in the basic composition of the matter. Such a change is known as physical change.

Interesting Example

Q. What happens to wood when it burns ?

A. It changes into ash.

Q. Can we change this ash into wood again ?

A. No we can't.

Q. Is the weight of the ash equal to that of wood ?

A. It looks much less.

Q. What happens to phosphorous when it is kept in air.

A. It burns and is converted into phosphorous pentaoxide.

Q. Can we change phosphorous pentaoxide into phosphorus ?

A. No, we can't.

Q. Is the weight of the phosphorus pentaoxide equal to that of phosphorus ?

A. It looks much less.

Teacher statement—In these examples we see that there is a change in not only its physical properties such as shape, size etc., but also its composition changes, is called a chemical change.

2. **Formulating Interesting Examples**

An interesting example is the one which arouses pupils' curiosity and interest. An interesting example secures and sustains pupils' attention which plays an important role in pupil learning. The term 'interesting' is a relative one. An example which is interesting to VI grade may not be interesting to XII grade pupils. A teacher, while formulating interesting examples, should always take into consideration the age level, grade level and the level of maturity of pupils.

3. Formulating Relevant Examples

An example is relevant which is related to the concept being explained. A relevant example helps pupils to understand the concept. On the other hand, an irrelevant one distracts pupil attention. At times, it even confuses them. This hinders their understanding of the concept of generalization. It is, therefore, essential that a teacher should use relevant examples.

A teacher should know various types of examples and its characteristics and keep them in mind while formulating examples for illustrating a particular concept or generalisation.

REINFORCEMENT

The term reinforcement represents a general category of events, perhaps much too broad for thinking about educational problems. Humans must have observed way back in pre-history that certain events that followed behaviour changed the probability of that behaviour occurring. These events have long been called rewards and punishments. Thorndike used the terms satisfiers and annoyers to describe these events ; but Skinner finds that such terms are so similar to ordinary language that they tend to incorporate meanings that they should not incorporate. He prefers to use the term reinforcers. This is a quite neutral term in that it does not imply that the event produces subjective pleasure or upset. Thus a reinforcer is simply an event which, following a behaviour, changes the probability that that behaviour will occur on a subsequent occasion.

Primary and Secondary Reinforcers

A distinction is commonly made between primary and secondary reinforcers. The point has already been made that certain conditions appear to f unction as reinforcers without any learning taking place. Food will reinforce the behaviour of a hungry animal. Every professional animal trainer, as well as the amateur training his dog, knows that food can be used to produce learning. Water will do the same for a thirsty animal, and so will any condition that satisfies a basic physiological need. Such a reinforcer is known as a primary reinforcer. Secondary reinforcers are stimuli that did not originally reinforce behaviour but that have acquired this property by having been associated with primary reinforcer. A secondary reinforcer may lose its power after it has been used for some time without being paired with the original reinforcer through which it acquired its reinforcing properties.

Just as one can identify clearly some events (such as food and water) that are primary reinforcers in their origin so, too, can one identify some events that are essentially secondary reinforcers. The giving of money is one of the most universally effective of secondary reinforcing events. However, just as tastes for particular foods are often acquired, and hence some foods under some conditions may function as secondary reinforcers, so too may money be valued by the adult partly because that same adult as a child liked to play with shining coins, and the response to bright objects may be largely an unlearned response. The so-called primary reinforcers may have primary components.

Positive Reinforcement

Positive reinforcement as used in situations in which responses are strengthened and positive approach behaviour is produced in the learner. For example children who respond well to praise. If the behaviours that elicit praise are related to school learning then the school learning of children responsive to praise may be enhanced. For these children the praise will have the effect of maintaining learning.

Negative Reinforcement and Punishment

There are conditions that the learner seeks to avoid. These are referred to in operant psychology as aversive conditions created through withholding of an expected reward. Teachers and parents commonly undertake the latter by taking away a child's privileges. Thus a child may be punished by not being allowed to go out to play. The withholding of a reward is generally believed to be an effective means of controlling behaviour. An interesting point to note is that while the withholding of an expected reward is punishing, the withholding of an expected punishment has not been established to have a consistently rewarding effect.

All aversive stimuli that actually occur may have two effects. They may inhibit behaviour at onset, that is at the time when they are immediately applied, but when they stop, the certain may have much of the effect of a reward. When one obtains relief from pain, the relief may have many of the consequences of positive reinforcement. Behaviours occurring at the time when an aversive stimulus ceases are strengthened. This is the phenomenon referred to as negative reinforcement. A negative reinforcer is a stimulus, the removal of which increases the strength of a response.

In the presence of an aversive stimulus, the organism typically shows escape behaviour. When an escape behaviour is successful, it reduces or removes the aversive stimulus. When this happens, the effective response is reinforced by the reduction or removal of the stimulus. The reinforcement thus operating is negative reinforcement.

Punishment must be distinguished from negative reinforcement. Punishment is used in society for the purpose of either weakening or obliterating a response. Negative reinforcement occurs when an aversive stimulus is turned off but punishment has its effect when an aversive stimulus is turned on. A situation involving punishment is one in which an aversive stimulus either accompanies or follows a learned response. In practice punishment and positive reinforcement are used in combination. Let us consider a situation in which a parent is watching a child play in front of yard. Each time the child shows signs of moving out into the street, the parent voices some mild threat that punishment is designed to inhibit the response of running out into the traffic. The child also discovers that as soon as he settles down again to play in the yard the threats of the parent are turned off. The withdrawal of a threat, like the termination of any other aversive stimulus, has the effect of strengthening the response that accompanies it. In this case, the response associated with the turning off of the aversive stimulus is that of playing in the front yard and hence this response is strengthened by the negative reinforcement. Punishment is likely to be most effective when it leads to an alternative and more desirable response that is strengthened by the turning off of the punishment.

Mowrer distinguishes punishment learning from learning that involves negative reinforcement in this way : "It is proposed that so-called punishment be termed passive avoidance learning (learning to avoid by not doing something) and that the contrasting form of avoidance learning (learning to do something as a means of avoidance) be termed active avoidance learning. The distinction is convenient one.

Schedules of Reinforcement

There are a vast number of different ways in which reinforcements can be arranged. Important are given below :

1. *Fixed-Ratio Schedule* : One may decide to reinforce every second, every third, or every fourth instance of the behaviour with which one is concerned. This is called a fixed-ratio schedule of reinforcement. After each reinforced response there are a number of non-reinforced responses before the next one is reinforced. Sometimes an abbreviation is used in discussing a fixed-ratio schedule. For example, if the sixth response and no other were to be reinforced, the term FR-6 would be used to indicate that a fixed ratio schedule was used and that every sixth response in the category of interest was reinforced.

2. *Variable Ratio Schedule* : In setting up such a schedule, the experimenter may decide that 25 per cent of the behaviours are to be reinforced, but that the number of non-reinforced behaviours that lie between two reinforced behaviours may vary from zero to eight. The number of non-reinforced trails between successive reinforced trails may be determined by throwing dice or by other means of obtaining a list of random numbers. The variable ratio schedule under consideration would be denoted as VR-4 to indicate that, on the average, one behaviour in four is reinforced.

Fixed Interval and Variables Interval Schedules

The Fixed Interval and the Variable Interval Schedule of reinforcement may be established not in terms of the number of consecutive behaviours that are non-reinforced following each one that is reinforced, but in terms of the time that elapses from one reinforcement to the next. One might decide, for example, to reinforce a child for the first occurrence of attentive behaviour following the end of five minutes period measured from the last attentive behaviour that was reinforced. If one did this, the reinforcement schedule would be described as a Fixed Interval Schedule or in this case, a FI-5 schedule. Finally, the interval of time between reinforcements may be varied and form a random pattern. When this is done, the interval is said to be a Variable Interval Schedule.

PROBING THROUGH QUESTIONS

Although evaluation questions represent the highest order of complexity, some attention should be directed to these problem questions used as a starting point for most instructional methods. Problem question is an open-ended one that implies a needed change from the *status quo*. It often begins with the word 'What', but may begin with such key-words as 'Why' or 'How'. The words 'Should' or 'Ought' are also implied in the question. For example, "What action should be taken to provide compensatory education for minority groups ?"

A problem of policy is most effectively treated when certain definable steps are followed. Each instrumental method has its own unique problem-solving approach. Each level of questioning, previously described, usually will be employed. To illustrate from the above example :

1. What is meant by compensatory education ? (recall question).
2. Why is compensatory education needed ? (comprehension question).
3. What assumptions are made about the benefits of compensatory education and minority groups ? (analysis question).
4. What is your judgement concerning the availability of compensatory education ? (evaluation question).

Several or even all questioning levels may be employed in each phase of the problem-solving process. Greater emphasis will be placed on certain questions at each level. Problem questions must be carefully pre-planned. If such questions are conceived, the subsequent problem-solving experience is of limited value. The most common error results from confusion between evaluation questions and questions of policy. An evaluation question tends to deal with one possible solution to a problem, whereas a policy question opens the door to any number of possible solutions. In the preceding illustration, for example, one possible solution could be to make compensatory education a pre-school requirement for all minorities. Sometimes the teacher, due to his or her own advanced understanding and biases, may word the problem as an evaluation-type question. To illustrate, "Should compensatory education be made a pre-school requirement for all minorities ?" Under such conditions, discussion tends to be limited to the merits and limitations of the one proposal. Some issues, of course, may have developed to the point that the adoption or rejection of a proposed course of action is all that must be resolved. In this case, a debate is in order. Evaluation questions, however, seldom provide an appropriate setting for discussion and related methods.

5

INNOVATIVE PRACTICES

MICRO-TEACHING

The destiny of our country is now being shaped in our classrooms. Teachers are said to be builders of a nation. Students of today are citizens of tomorrow. Among them would be teachers, doctors, engineers, scientists and leaders and from among them the most important role is that of teachers. It is very important for teachers to see that the subject matter which they teach is at every level interestingly taught by adoptiong the new techniques of teaching.

"The quality of training institutions remains, with a few exceptions, either mediocre or poor. Competent staff are not attracted. Vitality and realism are lacking in the curriculum and programme of work which continues to be largely traditional and set patterns and rigid techniques are followed in practice teaching with a disregard for present day needs and objectives" (Education Commission, 1966).

What we, teacher educators, teach in the class is different from the real school classroom situation. What methods we ask our student teachers to adopt while teaching, we rarely practise. It is not the general practice for teacher educators/method masters who take no classes in school to have a first hand experience of the difficulties faced by our students in the class.

Observation of student teachers during practice teaching is haphazard and is highly disappointing. A supervisor sits in the class generally for five to seven minutes and writes certain unspecific remarks like 'blackboard work is not good', 'do not be nervous, questioning is lacking etc. A supervisor does not have time even to discuss these remarks with the teacher. In some cases, the supervisor does not know the subject. The supervisory remarks are in global terms and do not pinpoint the mistake. For example one student teacher is teaching "Hard and Soft Water" just by lecture method and the supervisory remark is: Please make use of teaching aids/activities. This remark does not convey much. It would have been better if the supervisor had suggested that the activity of more lather formation on addition of soap solution to soft water and less with hard water, should be shown in the class. But such remarks are given only by a very few supervisors That is why it becomes very difficult for student teachers to incorporate the suggestions in subsequent lessons. A big gap exists between the student teacher and the supervisor who is generally the teacher educator. These develops on atmosphere of tension and artificiality during practice teaching. The result is that the majority of student teachers develop unfavourable attitudes towards practice teaching. It becomes boredom for them. They just want to complete the specified number of teaching lessons without their own satisfaction, without the satisfaction of the students and of the teacher educators.

Teahing is a very complex act. It is both art and science. Questioning, explaining, illustrations with examples, rewarding by accepting pupil responses, smiling making movements and gestures, looking into the eyes of the pupils, are some of the teaching behaviours generally expected from a teacher. The complexity of the problem can be reduced by breaking it up into simpler problems and aiming at one single and simple goal at a time and can be practised in simulated conditions. The National Council for Teacher Education while preparing the education curriculum has suggested practice teaching by student teachers in simulated conditions before they face the real classroom situation. It would be of definite advantage if a student teacher is put through a series a simulating micro-teaching situations before he is pushed into an actual classroom.

History

Micro-teaching was developed in the centre for Research and Development at Standford in 1960s. For its developmental history abroad, we can refer to Allen and Ryan, Turney, Brown,

Passi and Singh. The first impression that emerges from the study of the developmental history of micro-teaching abroad is that it is a technique based on high technology involving the use of sophisticated gadgets like Video Tape Recorder (VTR) and Closed Circuit Television (CCTV) for modelling the behaviour of student teacher in the use of particular skill and for providing feedback on his teaching perfomance. Even pupils drawn from the school to serve as pupils for micro-teaching sessions are paid in dollars and pounds. This situation created a dilemma for the developing countries, where neither the sophisticated technology nor resources for its introduction appear to be a reality in the near future. That is why, the innovation remained a far cry in teacher training in the developing countries despite the evidence to support its effectiveness in developing teaching competence in trainees as compared to the conventional programme of student teaching. Unless the technique is modified to suit the conditions available in the developing countries, its functional utility in their context is likely to remain a dream reality.

In the Centre of Advanced Study in Education (CASE), Baroda, interaction analysis using live observation without the aid of gadgets was being successfully experimented upon to study teacher behaviour and training of teachers in 1970s under the leadership of Prof. M.B. Buch. This provided a cue to adapting micro-teaching to the conditions prevailing in our teacher training institutions. So experimental try-out of micro-teaching with no technology or low technology was carried out at CASE, Baroda. Modelling was tried out through written material lectures, demonstration and discussion. Feedback was also based on systematic live observation. The results were encouraging. Micro-teaching was found to be more effective than the conventional programme of student teaching in developing different component teaching skills (Chudasama, Passi and Shah, Singh, Abraham, Joshi, Lalitha, Passi). Some work was also done in the Technical Teacher Training Institution.

The Department of Teacher Education in the National Council of Educational Research and Training designed a comprehensive project to study the effectiveness of micro-teaching in 1975 in collaboration with CASE. The experiment involving institutions from different parts of the country supported the results of the earlier studies. Simultaneously organisational problems of training colleges were assessed. The project was followed by research and developmental activities. A series of research projects to study the effectiveness of variations in micro-teaching components were taken up. Research and training programme, for teacher educators were initiated in collaboration with the Department of Education, University of Indore. The research studies produced empirical evidence for modifying micro-teaching procedure to suit the Indian conditions and the training of teacher educators provided persons for trying out, adopting and helping diffusion of the innovation.

Definition

Micro-teaching has been defined in different ways. It is not possible to reproduce all the definitions of micro-teaching. Some selected definitions will be examined.

Allen defined micro-teaching as "a scaled down teaching encounter in class size and class time".

He emphasises that micro-teaching is real teaching which has been scaled down in class size and class time. The number of students is generally from 5 to 10 and the duration of period ranges from 5 to 20 minutes.

David B. Young defined micro-teaching as "a device which provides the experienced teacher alike new opportunities to improve teaching". He further adds that it is a real teaching scaled down in time and size of the class. A micro-teaching sequence consists of preparing and teaching a 5 to 20 minutes' lesson to 1 to 5 students. The students are of the same age and ability etc., that he normally teaches.

M.B. Buch has given a comprehensive definition of Micro-teaching as "a teaching procedure in which teachers apply clearly defined teaching skills to carefully prepared lessons in planned series of 5 to 10 minutes encounters with a small group of real students, often, with an opportunity to observe the results on videotape".

Though Allen and Rayen have not given a formal definition of the term micro-teaching but they have specified the essential propositions of micro-teaching as follows:

1. Micro-teaching is real teaching but complexities of normal classroom are simplified.

2. There is emphasis on training for the accomplishment of specific task.
3. There is increased control of practice.
4. Normal knowledge of results or feedback dimension is greatly expanded.

In short micro-teaching can be described as a system of controlled practices that makes it possible to concentrate on a specific teaching behaviour and to practise teaching under controlled conditions. It requires the student teacher to teach a single concept using specified teaching skill to a small number of pupils in a short duration of time *i.e.* it is a scaled down process. It can be considered as a *miniaturised classroom.*

It should be remembered that micro-teaching is not a subsitute for general teaching rather it supplements it. The most important point in micro-teaching is that teaching is practised in terms of definable, observable, measurable and controllable teaching skill. When any act or behaviour attains the stage of saturation, it becomes a skill. A teaching skill is a set of teacher behaviours which are especially effective in bringing about desired change in pupils. A number of skills have been identified which are necessary for better teaching.

Some of the teaching skills are given below :

1. Skill of stimulus variation.
2. Skill of set induction.
3. Skill of closure.
4. Skill of teacher silence and non-verbal cues.
5. Skill of reinforcement.
6. Skill of recognising and attending questions.
7. Skill of explaining.
8. Skill of probing questions.
9. Skill of illustrating with examples.
10. Skill of increasing pupil participation.
11. Skill of blackboard writing.
12. Skill of class management.
13. Skill of writing instructional objectives.
14. Skill of using audio-visual aids.
15. Skill of pacing the lesson.

It is very difficult to expect all these teaching behaviours from a beginner student teacher. The task can be made easy if a students teacher is asked to practise these skills one at a time until optimisation is attained and can be achieved by adopting 'Micro criteria approach'. These skills can later on be synthesised during normal classroom teaching.

Operations in Micro-teaching

Micro-teaching provides an opportunity to teacher-trainee or experienced teacher to acquire new teaching skills and to refine old ones. It is a new technique which has been very successfully used in teachers training programmes. It involves various operations for its success. The operations are detailed below :

The first operation is the analysis of a skill in behavioural terms. The trainee is made clear about the objectives of the skill. The second operation involves the demonstration of the skill on videotape or films, or in normal classroom teaching.

The next important operation is that the trainee plans a short lesson in the subject of his interest in which he can use the skill.

The trainee teaches the lesson to a small group of student (5 to 10) which is videotaped or audiotaped.

Feedback is provided to the student teacher by videotape or audio-tape records who observes and analyses his lesson with the help of supervisor. The supervisor makes reinforcing remarks where the student-teacher used the skill effectively and points out the situations where the skill would have been exercised. The feedback and supervisor's remarks provide an insight to the student-teacher. He re-plans the lesson in order to use the skill more efficiently second time. The revised lesson is retaught to different but comparable groups.

Feedback is again provided on the retaught lesson which is analysed with the help of the supervisor.

Procedure of Micro-teaching

The micro-teaching technique consists of five steps of teach, feedback, re-plan, re-teach and re-feedback. In this technique one student teacher is teaching and the other is behaving as a peer supervisor and the remaining students behaving as peer pupils.

One research study shows that the class size in a micro-lesson can be safely increased from 10 students to 15 without affecting the competence to be gained by the students in the micro-teaching lesson. So where the strength of method masters in a training college is not sufficient, the student teachers can be given the training in micro-teaching by making a group of 15 in place of 10 which is the standard class size in micro-teaching technique. The main components of micro-teaching are discussed below :

1. *Teach* : A student teacher teaches a small class of 5-10 pupils. Pupils may be real pupils or his own class-fellows (peers) behaving as students of a lower desired standard. The time period is from 5-10 minutes. Time of six minutes is taken as standard in standard micro-teaching technique. The content of the lesson is a single concept. A micro-lesson is planned carefully so as to involve all the components of the skill to be practised. The lesson is observed either by the college supervisor or by a peer supervisor using a specially developed evaluation proforma for the skill or the lesson may be recorded on a video/audiotape if possible for later evaluation. The session is known as teach session.

2. *Feedback* : On the basis of observation, the student teacher is given the feedback immediately by the supervisor. The feedback is specific and not in global terms. The student teacher alongwith the supervisor goes out to a different room to discuss the performance. The source of the feedback may be self, or pupils, or peer supervisor, or video/audio recording or with the help of the observation proforma etc. But in our conditions, feedback by video/audio recording does not seem to be feasible. So feedback by peer supervisor or college supervisor is considered to be most suitable and is found to be equally effective. This session is called feedback or critique session and is also of 6 minutes.

3. *Replan* : During this session the trainee goes to another room where he replans or restructures his lesson in the light of the feedback received by him. This session is known as replan or restructure session and is of 12 minutes.

4. *Re-teach* : Next is the re-teach session where the trainee reteaches to a different set of pupils of the same unit or to the same

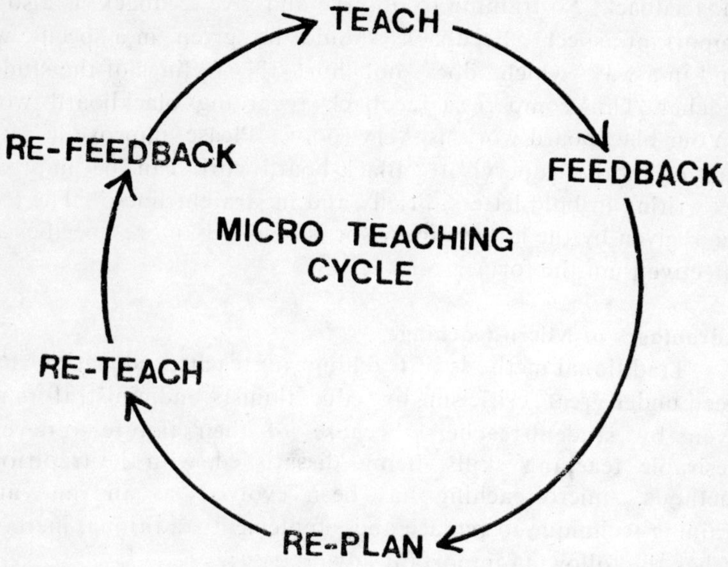

Showing Micro Teaching Cycle

set of pupils a different unit supervision of the lesson goes on as in the teach session. This session is also of 6 minutes.

5. *Re-Feed-back* : After reteach session there is refeedback regarding the lesson. This session is termed as refeedback or recritrique session and is of 6 minutes.

The five sessions put together constitute one micro-teaching cycle and gets completed in 36 minutes. This cycle may continue till the trainee attains perfection in that particular skill. The time period in the above sessions is flexible and may be changed a bit if so required depending upon local conditions.

Observation and Feedback

Planning of the lesson for a particular skill and its execution in teach and reteach session are very important components of micro-teaching. But equally important is observation of the lesson by the supervisor and feedback given to the student teacher in specific terms on the basis of the observations. In micro-teaching the class-fellow of the student teachers will be behaving as a supervisor. The role of the supervisor is very important, as the supervisor is a resource person for the student teacher. He is an adviser, assessor, morale booster and interpreter of feedback. So training to observe and give feedback is also an important aspect. Feedback should be given in a specific way and in a way which does not hurt the feelings of the student teacher. Thus compare a feedback regarding blackboard work, "Your blackboard work is very poor. Please improve it", with that of another supervisor, "Black-board work can be improved by writing in bold letters, briefly and in straight lines." The feedback given by the latter supervisor is definitely more specific and effective than the former one.

Advantages of Micro-teaching

Traditional methods of teaching in teacher education have been under great criticism by educationists, administrators and even by student-teachers because of their failure to develop desirable teaching skills. Being dissatisfied with the traditional methods, micro-teaching has been evolved as an innovative training technique to replace and supplement traditional methods. It has the following important advantages :

1. It is a teaching in a relatively simple and non-threatening context. It is simple because only one skill is selected for practice and non-threatening because the number of students is hardly 5 to 10.
2. The student teacher can focus his attention on clearly defined aspects of his behaviour.
3. There is provision for much fuller and more objective feedback to the trainee than in other teacher training procedure.
4. The teacher can experiment with several alternatives with a limited number of students each time with the opportunity for immediate evaluation and additional trials.
5. The micro-teaching sequence proves most effective when one as two teaching skills are selected for emphasis.
6. The student teacher can concentrate on some specific aspects of teaching-learning,
7. The micro-teaching focuses on individual task so that the teacher gets a very clear idea about the topic and the reaction it makes on the small group.
8. Patterns of classroom interaction and communication between the teacher and the students can be objectively and easily studied,

9. The objectives of micro-teaching are specified in terms of behavioural outcomes.
10. Individual micro-lessons are observed by other teachers and improvements can be suggested by them.

All the activities in micro-teaching set up can be recorded. Tapes (including videotape) of excellent teachers can be heard or viewed.

Comparison Between Traditional Teaching and Micro-teaching

Traditional teaching	*Micro-teaching*
1. Objectives are not specified in behavioural terms.	Objectives are specified in behavioural terms, class is divided into small groups of 5 to 10.
2. The class consists of 50 to 100 student teachers.	Class is divided into small groups of 5 to 10.
3. Teaching becomes complex and threatening.	Teaching is relatively simple and non-threatening.
4. Feedback is not immediately provided.	Immediate feedback is provided.
5. The role of the supervisor is vague and is not helpful to improve teaching.	The role of the supervisor is specific and well defined to improve teaching.
6. Patterns of classroom interaction cannot be objectively studied.	Patterns of classroom interaction can be objectively studied.
7. Student-teacher practises whole complex teaching behaviour.	Student-teacher practises only one skill selected for practice.
8. Time duration is 45 to 60 minutes.	Time duration in 5 to 10 minutes.

Many universities in India and abroad have adopted this technique in training colleges and the micro-teaching lessons are given due weightage in internship or practice teaching.

The difficulty of interaction of skills at the time of micro-lessons can be overcome by having mini-lessons in the beginning.

To start with, the lesson may be of 20 minutes duration involving 2-3 skills in one lesson. After having practice in such a mini course the student teachers may be asked to face the real classroom situation in macro-lesson of 35-40 minutes. By now, the student teacher will develop the skill of using the right time in his lesson.

Thus micro-teaching can be safely adopted in colleges of education for preparing better teachers without involving any extra expenditure. This technique can also be applied on in-service teachers. The skill which teachers are lacking may be identified and they may be trained only in those particular skills. Experiments in this direction have been done on school teachers in Bhopal, Delhi and other places and the results have been found to be very encouraging.

PROGRAMMED LEARNING

Programmed learning is the outcome of experiments of operant conditioning on pigeons in Skinner's laboratory in Harvard University. This concept arose from psychology not from technology. B.F. Skinner (1954) Professor of Psychology developed the operant conditioning theory of learning. He attended the opening day of his daughter's school and found that most of the classroom teachings were not satisfactory or effective. He tried to apply his theory for effective teaching and learning. He developed an Operant Conditioning Model of teaching and also published an article "Science of Learning and Art of Teaching" in 1954. His co-workers and associates gave momentum to programmed instruction concept. The application of Skinner's operant conditioning model is known as Linear Programming. In field of education programmed learning presented tremendous potentialities to meet the new challenges of the day.

Brief History

The development of technology of instructional process is a recent one. In pre-industrial phase of both education and industry, while industry was at the handwork level, the educational process relied upon devices like slate, black-board, chalk, etc. Industrial Revolution took place in industrial field in the beginning of 19th century but no such thing took place in case of education and instructional technology remained at the pre-industrial level. During the last quarter of 19th century there was some indication of incipient change in educational field. Liver reported that an International Exhibition was held in Vienna in 1873 in which an Exhibitant from American School with maps, charts, textbooks and other equipments gained much admiration of people and subsequent exhibitions in Paris (1878) and in Melbourne (1980) marked the imitation of instructional technology in field of education.

By 1900 industry had established factories and had begun to apply research and developmental concepts. Since 1900 to 1950 technology washed lightly upon the shores of instruction. Specific instances of American education may be cited in this context. By 1950, it had acquired the potentiality of a mass production technology. Dr. Alvin C. Eurich and his associate Dr. Alexander J. Stoddard gave the instructional process of American education as a sharp push into mass production technology. At that time there was shortage of teachers. Education and educationists were surrounded with free from all the sides and new technology of instructional process was being evolved.

Programmed Learning and Programmed Instruction

These two terms, programmed learning and programmed instruction, are used interchangeably for the same meaning but there is some difference. Programmed instruction and programmed learning have the same distinction as is between teaching and learning. It is evident from these two terms that there are two faces of a coin. These definitions are overlapping to some extent.

Term programmed learning concerns with the students activities. It can be characterised in terms of the learner's activities with the programmed material or teaching machines. Following are the basic principles of programmed learning :

1. Learner works individually at his own rate with teaching machine.
2. The learner through a carefully ordered sequence of material which ask him to respond in some way or the other.

3. The matter is so designed that the students make few errors.
4. At every step the learner is informed if his response is right or wrong.

The term programmed instruction is concerned with activities of teacher or programmer. It can be enumerated in terms of what teachers do in preparing programmed material. Following are the basic steps of programmed instruction—

1. Objectives of the programme are identified precisely. These are written in behavioural terms. Learner will be able to perform when he had gone through the programmed text.

2. The entering behaviours are specified in terms of previous knowledge, skills and objectives of the students using the programmed material.

3. The programmed material to be taught and the skills to be developed in the learner are analysed thoroughly.

4. This analysis determines :

 (a) Optimum instructional sequence
 (b) Appropriate instructional strategies
 (c) Appropriate device of presentation.

5. The programmed matter is tried, revised and validated on basic empirical data of students performances.

6. The programmed matter is evaluated on students for whom the programmed matter is designed.

It is evident from above principles that designer proceeds from logical sequence of the continent elements to the psychological sequence of the content which shows the effectiveness of the instructional materials.

Definition of Programmed Learning

B.F. Skinner has defined programmed learning as a method of designing reproducable sequence of instructional events to produce a measurable and consistent effect on behaviour of each and every acceptable student.

In short programmed learning may be defined as "designing a strategy in which various kinds of intellectual, emotional and motor experiences are provided to learners in a controlled situation through a variety of devices like a book, machine, teacher, radio and television. In programmed learning the designer has to follow the laws of science of behaviour and prove the validity of the strategy in terms of student's learning.

Components of Programmed Learning

There are four components of programmed learning which are as follows :

1. Instructional goals; the system of objectives.
2. The entering behaviour, the system of input of assumptions of learning.
3. The instructional procedures, the system of operation or sequence of content.
4. Performance assessment, terminal behaviour or output monitor.

Characteristics of Programmed Learning

On the basis of above discussions the following characteristics can be concluded.

1. Controlled presentation of matter.
2. Elicitation of appropriate response.
3. Guidance with respect to the subject matter.
4. Control over the way in which learning proceeds.
5. Constant assessment of performance.

Thus this is an individualised technique of instruction which presents the subject matter stepwise in logical order. This method has following advantages :

1. It makes use of teaching principles which have been known for years in crowded classroom.
2. Immediate feed-back is given to the learner.
3. Objectives are pin-pointed and are specially defined in operational terms.
4. Programmer organises subject matter systematically and presents it with great care and precision.
5. Student is forced to participate actively by making continuous responses.
6. Programme is developed empirically through a series of

tryouts on typical students and is repeatedly refined with effective sequences of frames being retained and ineffectives being discarded.

Objectives of Programmed Learning

Following are important objectives of programmed learning.

1. To help the learner to learn at his own pace.
2. To help the learner to learn independently without a teacher.
3. To help for self study and to assess his performance himself by comparing it with the given answers.
4. To present the learning material in a logical and sequential manner.

Principles of Programmed Learning

At the beginning the principles of programmed learning were identified and formulated by B.F. Skinner. These principles imply the rules and systems by which a programmed instruction material function and is constructed. These principles have been divided into following three categories :

1. Fundamental principles of programmed learning.
2. Basic principles of programmed learning.
3. The mandatory and optional principles of programmed learning.

Fundamental Principles

Good programmed Instruction nearly incorporates good principles of learning. In programmed learning the subject matter is resolved into different steps. The sequence and the steps must be determined carefully and skilfully. The steps must be small enough for the learner to go ahead easily with minimum errors. The trial and error learning must be reduced to minimum. Ideal result will lead to no mistake. Constant success reinforces the past learnings and motivates for further efforts. Programmed learning type depends on the subject and desired objectives. One common type in academic subjects is to present certain carefully worded datas in a framer viewing space. Each frame calls for a response. The response may be written or selected among the given alternatives.

The basic idea of programmed learning is "the most efficient, pleasant and permanent learning." Programmed learning has many features, different from conventional method of teaching. The basic principles of programmed learning were discovered in psychological laboratories.

1. Principle of small steps : The subject matter to be programmed is analysed thoroughly and divided into meaningful segments of information. These segments are presented one at a time to learner and are called "Frames".

2. Principle of Active Responding : For learning, learner must respond. Programming helps in active response made by the learner and induces sustained activity. While working on a programme, learner remains busy and active. A good programme requires the thorough understanding of previous frames by moving to next. Learner's active response means his involvement in learning process. It does not mean a little response for a little frame. A further confusion about active responding is overt and covert responding. Overt response means observable response and covert response means unobservable response. The idea that only overt response is active, is wrong. Both the type of response may be active provided that the learner participates actively in the learning process.

3. Principle of Immediate Confirmation : It is principle of immediate confirmation of results. When a learner proceeds through a linear programme, he is provided with the knowledge of results immediately after responding, he can compare his response with the correct response is confirmed and if he is wrong, he will read and correct his response so as to give correct response the next time when he is asked the same question. It is a truism that learning accompanied by success and satisfaction is likely to be more permanent than the learning accompanied by failure and dissatisfaction. B.F. Skinner in his teaching method devised a mechanism of controlling the learner's behaviour. The learner goes through each step, gives a response and receives immediate feedback of his performance.

4. Principle of Self-Pacing : Learner proceeds at his own pace, while working on a programme. He is forced to move with the other members of the class. Programming being provided with self pacing has incorporated the principle of individual difference in teaching and learning process.

5. Principle of Student Testing : Last and fifth principle of programming is student testing. The teacher can regularly assess the progress of his student. He can find out the weakness of his programme and with the help of students performance he can make corrections in his programmes. The students can themselves evaluate their performance on the programmes.

Steps to work on the Programme : The learner can easily work on the principles of programming and remember the important features of programmed learning by remembering five key-words :

Principle	Function	Symbol
1. Small steps	Reading	R
2. Active responding	Writing	W
3. Immediate confirmation	Checking	C
4. Self pacing	Advancing	A
5. Student testing	Record or testing	T

First read the stepwise material, then write the answers, which are your responses. Next confirm your answer. Since the confirmation of response is made immediately, the principle of immediate confirmation has been used. After confirmation of correctness of response we can proceed at our own speed which reminds of principle of self pacing. The detail record which the student leaves provides the basis for revision of programme. This is the principle of student testing.

Basic Principles of Programmed Learning

Following are the basic principles of programmed learning :

1. Objective specification : It means identification of terminal behaviours which the learner will be able to perform after completing the programming. These are the intended outcomes rather than the mastery of the content.

2. Small step size : It includes the imparting of knowledge in smaller units. And each activity is reinforced.

3. Overresponding : It means students have to respond to each unit of information by means of exercises provided to assimilate.

4. Success or minimal error : Error must be avoided at any cost because these have been constructed for abstract learning.

5. *Immediate Feedback* : In order to ensure success the student must know whether his response is correct or not.

6. *Logical Graded Process* : It implies two things (i) relevance of content and (ii) its graded presentation.

7. *Self pacing* : It means that individuals move with their own pace and thus it allows the individualisation of instruction.

8. *Empirical Testing* : It is used for programme development and its validation. The programmed matter is prepared, modified and evaluated in terms of learner's performance.

These principles are formulated for the development of programmed instruction material and are based on B.F. Skinner's theory of behaviour.

Mandatory and Optional Principles of Programmed Learning

Optional and mandatory principles are those which may or may not be present in it. The mandatory principles are those which are critical and essential for distinguishing it from other forms of instruction like conventional classroom teaching by use of textbooks. According to Edward (1971) the following three are referred to as mandatory principles :

1. The principle of objective specification.
2. The principle of empirical testing.
3. The principle of self pacing.

He also mentioned the following three optional principles of programming in contrast with :

1. Principle of Overt responding,
2. Principle of immediate feedback.
3. Principle of small steps.
4. Principle of prompting and confirmation.

Programmed Learning Principles

1. Mandatory Principles : Principles of		2. Optional Principles : Principles of
(i) Objective specification	(a) Individual try-out	(i) Over responding
(ii) Empirical testing	(b) Small group try-out	(ii) Immediate feedback

(iii) Self pacing	(c) Field try-out	(iii) Small step size (a) Types of response. (b) Error rate (c) Sequence (d) Prompting and confirmation.

Steps of Designing a Programmed Instructional Material

By using following steps we can prepare the programmed instructional material quickly and easily :

1. Selection of unit according to your objective, ability; interests.
2. Preparation of comprehensive content outline of the topic carefully with the help of teachers (Content analysis).
3. Define objectives in behavioural terms and should specify the :

   (i) Generalised goal
   (ii) Programme objective
   (iii) Interm objective
   (iv) Probable pre-requisite skills or entering behaviour.

4. Device a strategy of learning where the students begin, which sequence of tasks would lead him most effectively towards goal, how much repetition is needed and the kindof illustration, etc.
5. Write series of frames stimulus response items by using following steps :

   (a) Present the material in frame. Frame a single step of programme usually containing information and questions to be answered in one form or the other. It indicates the learning of material presented.
   (b) Edit the frames for their accuracy of content, eligibility of language, correction of student response and carefully sequence of the frames based on discrimination, generalisation, contiguity, practice and reinforcement.

6. Re-editing of test and preparing draft for try-out.
7. Try-out the programme to know if the students make much errors or become confused at some point, if yes the draft should be revised carefully.
8. Evaluation and validation should be done by administering it on a representative group of students.
9. Final printing of the prepared programme shall be made.

Types of Programming

There are many types of programing for presenting the subject matter to learners. Four important types are given below :

(1) Linear or Extrinsic (2) Branching or Intrinsic
(3) Computer Assisted Instruction (4) Mathetics.

(1) *Linear or Extrinsic type* : This style of programming as have been already mentioned was developed by B.F. Skinner of Harvard University during his fifties. This is also called as the Skinnarian style of programming. The techniques associated with this type are based on the principle that learner's original response shall be gradually altered until he gets some standard of acceptable performances. Skinner believed that the behaviour of animals or human beings can be altered or modified when it is gradually changing in successive approximations. According to him the best way of teaching the students is to provide them with knowledge in small segments and writing them in such a way so that only correct responses are likely to occur. Students can learn faster if they succeed. They should be told about their performance at the moment. Then he will actively participate in learning process by responding soon. In Skinner's opinion recall response (constructed response) are more efficient in learning process than the recognition type of response. He believed the student's responses cause the teaching to occur.

He was fully convinced by the successful research studies on the behavioural modification of animals that even human beings can be led to the desired goal by presenting the subject matter in smaller steps, each step is provided with reinforcement or reward favourable experience. The reinforcement increases the probability of recurrence of correct responses. Take the example of hungry rat in Skinner's box. A good pallet to the rat at each time the buzzer sound. Any type of complex behaviour can be shaped through a stimulus response chain. Following *e.g.* will explain the process of chaining :

SD—→	R—→	SR—→	R—→	SR—→	R—→	SD
General Stimulus in chamber	Orient towards lever	Sligh of lever	Approach to lever	Contact with lever	Press lever	Food

When the principles of chaining is applied to human beings, it operationally works as a learner is present with a small amount of information and is asked to answer a question. As soon as he responds his response is confirmed serving as the reinforcer. Thus by continuous reinforcement of learner's behaviour, we can lead to the desired goal.

Features of Linear Type of Programming

All the fundamental principles of operant conditioning have been incorporated in the linear programming are briefly described as follows :

1. *Linear arrangement* : Linear means to proceed in a straight line. In linear programme, generally, all the learners advance in a single series of short steps which are designated to ensure a high rate of correct response to the frame. All the learners have to pass through the same fixed sequence of frames determined by the programmer only. The learner starts from his initial behaviour to the terminal or final behaviour in straight line sequence. Following diagram shows the working of linear programme :

Linear Model Sequence

2. *Controlled responses* : In linear type the responses are controlled by programmer. Learner has no choice of his own in responding.

3. *Emphasised response* : Here the emphasis is laid on response. The learner must respond to each and every frame for learning to occur.

4. *Immediate feedback* : The linear programme is designed

in such a way that he can immediately compare his response at the very moment with the response provided by the programmer at the left hand or the foot of the frame.

5. *Act prompting* : A prompt is an additional stimulus in the frame which helps the learner to respond correctly. In the beginning the programme prompts, hits and cues are introduced to avoid unnecessary wastage of time to find out correct response.

6. *Active participation* : Linear programme involves active participation of learner. He has to construct response for every frame.

7. *Self pacing* : Every learner proceeds at his own speed. He is not forced to proceed with the speed of other members.

8. *Linear programme may be used by children* of first grade because mechanism of linear programme is simple.

9. *Self constructed response* : In linear model the learner has to construct his own responses.

10. In linear type cheating is avoided by hiding of responses from the learner by means of some mechanical devices. Chart proof teaching machines have been developed through which self instructional programmed material can be presented to learner.

11. The linear programming style is best suited in subject areas where facts and information can be properly sequenced.

12. Stimulus discrimination (S.D.) is emphasised in linear programme.

13. There are some programmes which have been developed on linear model in which a learner can skip a certain no, of frames provided he responds correctly a test items at a particular frame. Such programme is called skiplinear programme.

1 ——→ 2 ——→ 3 ——→ 4 ——→ 5 ——→ 6 ——→ 7

Test item Skip to Frame No. 6

Limitations of Linear Style of Programming

Research workers developed most of the programmes of linear style and used them in actual classroom teaching. Generally all the workers have pointed out following limitations of Linear style of programming :

1. *Lack of Motivation* : It is alleged by most of the teachers

and students so learning becomes dull and monotonous because it is very much time consuming for teaching few simple points. For gifted children the material is without challenge and interest.

2. *No freedom of choice* : Learner has no choice of his response. It is alleged that creative imagination and learner's do not have to contribute their judgemental ability towards discovery of answers but have to follow the rigid line prescribed by writer.

3. Rothkopf's opinion was that in many linear programmes, the learner finds out the clue as to what is to be filled in the blank and key terms are guessed.

4. The linear style of programming as mentioned above can be used in limited areas where the subject matter can be properly sequenced such as science, mathematics and vocabulary development in languages.

5. Sidney L. Pressey criticised linear style of programming on following points :

(i) Serial order learning—The frames are presented in serial order and so the learning is also acquired in serial order, whereas learning in actual life is not always serial.

(ii) In linear style the subject matter is broken into smaller steps, and learner has not to do any searching for matter and the creative ability is inhibited.

(iii) Linear style does not permit any differentiation among responses.

6. Programmes are generally designed with the presumption that the learner is not supposed to have any previous knowledge of the students is very difficult.

7. In term of book from presentation the learners are expected to be honest but all of them cannot prove to be honest. They can see the correct response without frame.

Thelene's Criticism : H.A. Thelene in his book entitled *Programmed Materials Today* : *Critique and Proposal* (1963) has criticised the linear model on following points :

1. The notion that learner should be rewarded at each step is not proved. Many experiments similar to those of Skinner's studies on rat have shown that linear type is unguided and unrewarded learning.

2. If we assume that reward is necessary at each step then the question arises as how to give reward. The answer to it is to

make such steps the learner makes rare errors. The doubt is that continuous success is itself rewarding. Thelene reports that boredom sets in after first few hours of programmed instruction, seem to be a practical evidence.

3. The criterion of a good programmed instruction so far used is that it is free of errors but the relationship between this criterion and any educational criterion remain completely unestablished.

4. While the art of programming is concerned with developing an effective sequence of items, experiments have revealed that learners learn just as much with items presented in random order as they were presented in sequence by programmer.

5. Role of teacher is unspecified.

6. The same programme is used for all the students without considering the individual differences. Their requirements skills are same and the content is covered in same way.

7. Notion that active learning is better and that the machine require activity, is uncertain in its application to present programmes. Experiments have shown that there is no difference in learning when he responds actually or he merely reads the items.

8. There is no control over student's motives. His posture is extraordinarily docile and he is not expected to participate in goal setting.

9. The presently designed programmes are teacher proof and self contained. They can't deal with unanticipated or emergent feelings and ideas.

(2) *Branching or Intrinsic Style* : Second most popular and conventional style of developing programmes is branching. This style was originated by Norman A. Crowder and is called Crowderian style. This is also called as branching or intrinsic style of programming. It has been defined as "a programme which adopts to the needs of the students without the medium of extrinsic device, such as computer." This is called intrinsic because the learner has to make decisions himself to adopt the instruction to his needs according to his previous knowledge of the subject. The principle of branching style is that different students need different instructional materials and that students can learn from their own errors. This principle is quite different from linear programming in which all the students uniformally

follow the same sequence of frames irrespective of their previous knowledge of the subject.

The rationale of intinsic programming postulates that basic learning takes place during the exposure of students to new materials. Growder believes that learning is communication. He favoured larger chunks of material at a time which may convey a total concept to the learner. His technique of communication is quite different from Skinner's. In branching the student's choice determine directly and automatically the material he will follow in the programme.

Construction of branching programming

Practically there is no difference between linear and branching styles at preparatory stage of programme. At 2nd stage the information is not broken into smaller steps but is presented in larger steps. Mode of response is also different. The student has to select correct response out of four or five alternatives. The student is rooted through the branches according to his response. The paradigm appears like the following figure.

Main Stem

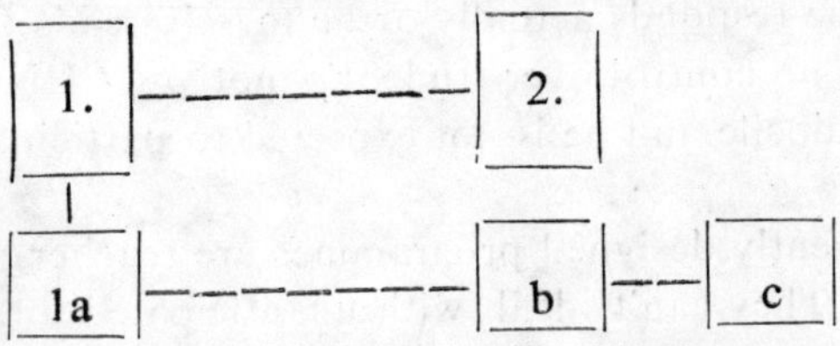

The procedure of writing frame sequence in developing a programme is different from that in the linear programme. There are two types of branches. Main stem and remedial frame. First the programmer should write the main sequence of frames with multiple choice answers, after that he should try it on a small group of target population and decide, which parts of the programme are likety to cause the greater amount of difficulty and require remedial subsequences.

Features of Branching Style

1. In branching programme, a frame is larger and more information is presented at each step. A step may convert of 2-3 paragraphs and sometimes a full page. The programmer has ample opportunity to export his literary style in presenting the subject in larger frames.

2. Multiple Choice questions are asked. Each response is keyed to different page. If the learner selects correct responses, it will be confirmed. If he fails in doing so he is routed to material which explains as why is he wrong. Formal is like the given figure :

————————

Information ————

————

————

Answer

1..................Page 4

2..................Page 10

3..................Page 20

4..................Page 30

3. Crowder holds that teaching is communication and so he concentrates his attention upon the improvement of communication.

4. Learner is free to choose his own path of action according to his previous knowledge of the subject.

5. Learners are more alert and carefully concentrate on subject matter. It is considered to be more challenging and interesting to students.

6. Detection and correction of errors is emphasised. Crowder permits 20% errors in his model. In such a model the errors are first detected and then corrected. Learner comes to know to eliminate errors in the process of learning.

7. The material presented to each student is continuously and directly controlled by the learner's performance is responding to questions.

8. When branching programmed material is presented in book form, the book is called a scrambled textbook, because the papers do not follow the normal sequence.

9. It has been proved by experimental studies that branching is very useful for concept learning. It leads itself best to learning situation involving a choice of solutions to a problem.

10. Role of active response is not central in intrinsic programming. It offers less guidance to the learner as to what material in the frame is important.

Limitations of Intrinsic Style

1. There is every possibility that the learner may guess the correct response without understanding the subject matter of the frame.

2. Infinite branching cannot be provided, because it does not satisfies the need of all individuals because it is very difficult to find out the total number of branches to every individual.

3. It is economically very costly due to costly audio-visual aids.

4. Programme needs revision after every 2 years.

5. Programmes are the product of a programmers imagination and it is he who decides diagnostic questions and level of content. The diagnostic questions may or may not suit the needs of learners.

6. Branching model can be used after class VI because small children cannot follow its mechanism.

7. It is very difficult to ask questions on the whole matter of a frame because frames are too large and sometimes important points are left out.

8. Some programmers doubt the acquisition of higher learning through branching programme sequences beyond the level of recognition.

9. In branching programme through the process of elimination all students may eventually get through the material. By simply looking at the programme knowledge can't be gained whether the student has comprehended the material; the fact that he has arrived at the last frame in the programme does not necessarily mean that he has learned the whole matter of programme.

10. It is unable to control the students. This technique does not shape the student's behaviour.

(3) *Computer Assisted Instruction* : Computer-assisted instruction (CAI) is a natural outgrowth of the application of the principles of programmed leaving. The origins of CAI could probably be linked with attempts made by some technicians to see if a machine could be programmed to

interact with a human being. In the beginning, very simple programmes were tried out on machines, such as printing of pre-stored questions, accepting multiple choice answers, and judging answers for correctness. First major work was done in 1961 at University of Illinois, when the programmed logic for automatic teaching operations were produced. The 2nd major work was done by Patrick Suppes at Stanford University in 1966, when the computerised tutorials in arithmatic and reading of elementary school children were developed.

Basic Assumptions of Computer Assisted Instruction

This system has been developed of assumption which have made it popular and acceptable in education and training at different levels and areas. It holds great potential for education of the future. Given below are some of the basic assumptions :

1. Computer assisted instruction can be arranged for 4000 students simultaneously.
2. In C.A.I. performance of each learner during the course and on the test is automatically recorded and can be feed-back to the teacher so that he may promptly evaluate the learner's performance and use the education in designing the best teaching strategy for learner's future.
3. This assumption relates the presentation of a variety of subject materials. It can be used in all types of teaching learning programmes.

CAI System and its Mechanism

Basically this system is described in terms of its 'hardware' (the machine), its 'software' (the programme), its communication links the devices (which allow the learners to use the hardware and software) and the curriculum of teaching material stored in a computer.

The C.A.I. system has been utilised at all levels of education, ranging from the elementary school to post-graduate and to the job training in almost all subjects. In following paragraph the actual operation of a C.A.I. programmed designed to teach reading it has been described. In C.A.I. system in an elementary school the child sits in front of a tube resembling T.V. screen and is capable of displaying message generated by the computer in the form of numbers, words or geometrical diagrams. There is a key board in front of the tube that the child can use to respond the problem shown on screen. The child also has a light pen which permits him to react to stimuli on the tube by touching a particular portion of the screen. Earphones and microphones are also available for communication between computer and child. Atkinson (1968) designed a programme for teaching the reading process to infants first he must learn to identify letters. This task is accomplished in three following stages of the programme.

First stage—A model letter appears on a projector connected with a computer, while 3 letters are presented on the screen. A recorded voice instructs the child to look at the better on projector and touch the same letter on the screen with light pen. Different letters are shown on the projector and the child is given training in the process of identification of a single letter. The task looks like the following figure :

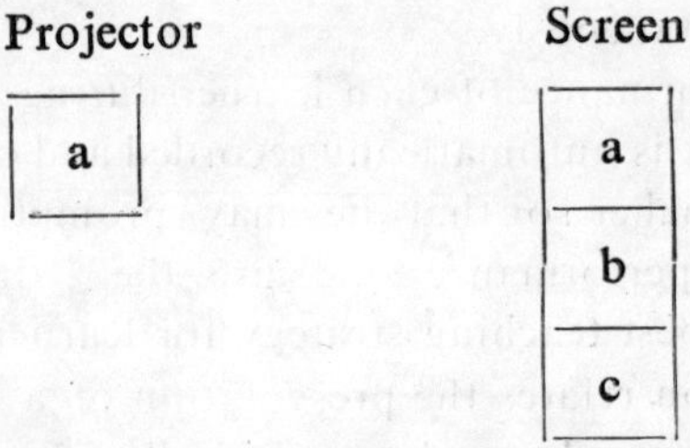

Second stage—Second phase begins after the mastery of a single letter identification. The child learns during 2nd stage to discriminate pairs of letters. The task book looks like the following figure :

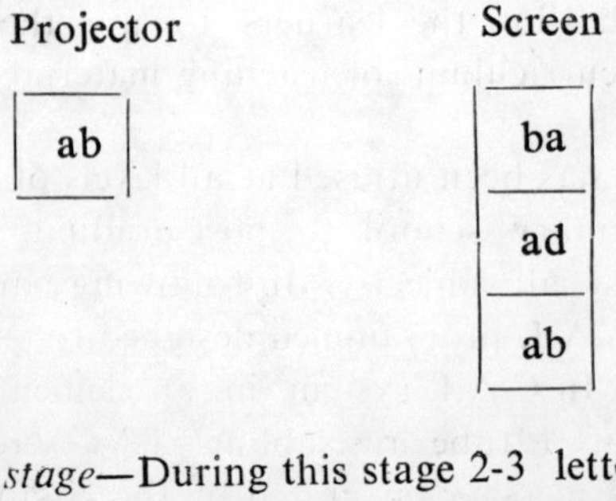

Third stage—During this stage 2-3 lettered combination are presented on screen and the child is instructed to touch 1 symbol out of the 2 combinations which are identical and the other symbol if they are different. The task would visually look like the figure given below :

Han	Hat
OO	O
Hall	Han
OO	O

Attaining mastery over letter identification independent of any association with sounds, the learner moves on towards identification of skills involving groups of words with similar sound and structure. A set of simple problems has the following form:

On

□

rat

bat

fan

ran

A recorded voice tells the child to touch and say the word that would be framed by combing the letters on the side and top of the square. If he touches the correct word, he sees its appearance on square cell. The voice comes that "ran" has appeared in the box and child has to touch it again. If he makes an error by touching a wrong word, the computer is programmed to show him, which of the following errors he has made :

(i) He picked the word with correct beginning but wrong ending (rat).

(ii) He picked the word with correct ending but wrong beginning (fan).

(iii) He picked the word with neither correct ending nor the beginning (bat).

The child then practice commensurate to his error. Exact records of the errors and success are automatically recorded so that all drills are tailored to meet his individual needs. The drills that various learners receive may be entirely different because different errors were made by different individuals.

After mastery in reading skill child proceeds to complex skills. The objective of their programme is to teach reading skill to child. Computers have been designed to store and retrive vast amount of information They can thus rapidly and effectively provide knowledge about the success and failure of learners on various parts of programme. But even the most enthusiastic proponents of C.A.I. do not believe that at present the computer is a complete tutor.

When a child encounters great difficulties and makes a little or no progress, a mechanism in the computer notifies the teachers, who provides the necessary attention to the learner. If similar difficulties are met by majority of learners then the computer programme is modified computer based instruction does not ignore the talents of human teacher but explores them to their fullest extent in a tutorial relationship. The complete system of C.A.I. is shown by diagram.

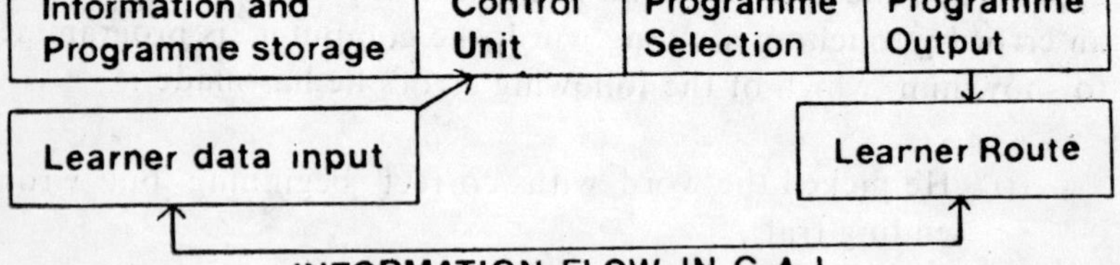

INFORMATION FLOW IN C.A.I.

Applications of C.A.I.—C.A.I. has wide range of application in almost every aspect of human life. A few prevalent of them are following :

1. *Administrative* C.A.I. has been used to keep records and processing data for research.

2. *Drill and Practice* C.A.I. is used for drill and practice

problem in science, mathematics and languages, etc. This computer has been an effective substitute of a teacher in this exercise. C.A.I. has been successfully used in mathematics, science, languages, business management, airforce and medical profession.

3. Simulation computers are used to simulate real life experience in medical science, biological sciences, airforce, business management, etc. to enhance the efficiency of the workers and improve the performance quality.

Limitations of C.A.I.—No doubt C.A.I. is becoming a great potential tool for education and training but it must overcome many handicaps which are inherent in its functioning. These are the following :

1. Speech or writing analysis by computer in a useful form seems to be a far off phenomenon.
2. Warmth and emotional climate created by a teacher in class by interacting with the students is absent in C.A.I.
3. C.A.I. programmes do not solve psychological or educational problems by themselves.
4. C.A.I. fails to develop essential features of language competency where the ability to construct or generate meaningful sentences is necessary.
5. C. A. I. cannot appreciate the students artistic endeavour.
6. Major problem in C.A.I. study is fatigue.

(4) *Mathetics* : Mathetics technique of programming was developed by F. Gilbert in 1962. He defined it as the "the systematic application of reinforcement theory to analysis and reconstruction of those complex behaviour repertories usually known as subject matter mastery, knowledge and skill______ mathetics, if applied diligently produces teaching materials that exceed the efficiency of lessons produced by any known method.

During preparation of a mathetical programme, normally the following five stages are followed :

(i) Data collection and task analysis (ii) Writing a learning prescription. (iii) Characterisation and lesson plan (iv) Frame or exercise writing (v) Editing.

An Example of a Mathetical Programme

The use of the process of chaining a mathetical programme is being given to acquaint the learner with the process of demonstration, promptation and reaction in an exercise. The process starts from the last operant in the chain and proceeds backward. This is not a test but a programme. Do whatever the programme ask. If you come to a blank(———) put the correct number. When a respose is required for you will find the correct response on lower part of the page. Check your response and go ahead.

1. To find the square of a 2-digit number ending in 5.

   A. Multiply the 1st digit by the next consecutive number.

   B. Write 25 to the right of the result.

No response required
Programme page 2.

2. To find the square of 25

   (A) Multiply the 1st digit (2) by the next higher consecutive (3)

   (B) Write 25 to the right of result (6)

   (C) The square of 25 is 625.

No response required
Programme page 3.

3. To find the square of 45

   (A) Multiply the first digit (4) by the next higher consecutive (5)=20.

   (B) Write 25 to the right of the result.

   (C) Square of 45 is 2025.

Programme page 4.

4. To find the square of 65

   (A) Multiply the 1st digit (6) by next higher consecutive

   (B) Write .... to the .... of the result.

   (C) The square of 65 is ....

   (B) Write 25 $7 \times 6 = 42$

   (C) Square of 65 is 4225

Programme page 5.

5. To find the square of 75

(A) Multiply ...... by.........

(B) Write.........to the......of.........

(C) The square of 75 is.........

(A) Multiply 7 by 8

(B) Write 25 to right of 56

(C) The square of 75 is 5625

Programme page 6.

6. What is the square of (A) 85 ? (B) 95 ?

7. 7225 9025 Programme page 7

Some disadvantages of Mathetical Programming

There are following disadvantages of mathetical programme :

1. It is a time consuming process.
2. This programme needs skill and competence so it is a highly complicated process.
3. The production cost of mathetical lessons is greater than for other types of programmes because of heavier use of illustrations.
4. Backward chaining is sometimes very difficult to apply in actual training situations.

Comparison of Programming Method After Patricia Calender (1969)

Item Methods	*Linear*	*Branching*	*Mathetics*	*Computerised instruction*
1	*2*	*3*	*4*	*5*
1. Unit of Presentation	1. The frame	1. The frame	1. The operant	1. May be linear or branching at lowest level of prog.
2. Step size	2 Small	2. Larger	2. As big as possible	2. Varies according to prog. selected by computer.
3. No. of steps	3. Large	3. Small	3. As few as possible.	3. Can be large or small
4. Response	4. Constructed	4. Multiple choice	4. Written or by performance task on simulator	4. Selection of appropriate response button
5. Error rate	5. 5%	5. Varies according to programme usually 20%	5. Some deliberate error written into prog. to sharpen discrimination.	5. Error rate variable

6. Reinforcement	6. Correctness of response	6. Ultimate correct as of response.	6. Task completion	6. Ultimate correctness of response
7. Sub. matter suitability.	7. Sub. which can be divided into small pcs	7. Where broader concepts or large pcs. of information can be given.	7. Suited to Kinaesthetic or discrimination skill	7. Complex sub-matter
8. Paper Prog.	8. Linear Book	8. Scrambled Text	8. Prog. instruction package	8. Punch card or take fed into the computer
9. Machine.	9. Simple linear	9. Film Programme	9. Simulation devices	9. Computer linked with electric type writer
10. Cost Paper	10. Printed on paper and quite costly	10. More expensive	10. High cost	10. High cost
11. Cost of Machine	11. Cheap	11. More than linear	11. Varies according to type of simulators	11. Very high

PANEL DISCUSSION

Panel discussion involves a group of five to eight persons who are seeking agreement on a problem of concern to themselves and to an audience. This technique was used by Herry A. Ober Street for the first time in 1929. He organized a discussion of a small group for definite period before an audience. At the end of the discussion audience had also participated. The important questions were put by the audience on the topic. The experts tried to answer the questions and certain points were clarified, which were not included in the discussion. Several other persons had used this technique later.

How Panel Discussion Differs from Class Discussion ?

Though the objectives of classroom discussion and panel discussion are same, the approaches are different. Some of the features that distinguish panels from class discussion are following:

1. The teacher directs the entire class in class discussion whereas a panel of students has control of the panel operation.
2. Preparation for class discussion is controlled to a large degree by the teacher, while the panel members plan and prepares for their discussion.
3. Class discussion, when used appropriately, involves the whole process of solving a problem; the panel group may discuss only one major aspect of the problem.
4. A class discussion leader is often a dominant, central figure, whereas the panel leader, is usually the quietest person on the panel.
5. Even in a balanced class discussion the amount of actual participation is limited, whereas all panel members have ample opportunity to participate.
6. Class discussion is controlled and directed by an authority figure who, by student standards, can be considered an expert. The panel, on the other hand, is led by one member of the peer group who is not an expert.

Objectives of Panel Discussion

The following are the main objectives of this technique :

1. To provide information and new facts.
2. To analyse the current problem from different angles.

3. To identify the values.
4. To organize for mental recreation.
5. To facilitate higher cognitive learning.

Principles of Panel Discussion

This technique is based on the following principles :

1. Equal opportunities be provided to every participant.
2. It must encourage the active participation with originality and independence.
3. It should involve feeling of cooperation and sympathy and respect to the ideas of others.
4. It be based on modern theory of organization.

Types of Panel Discussion

There are two types of panel discussion :

(a) Public panel discussion.
(b) Educational panel discussion.

(a) *Public Panel Discussion* : This type of panel discussion is organized for the common place problems felt by general public. The following objectives are achieved by this type of panel discussion :

(i) To provide factual information regarding current problems.
(ii) To determine the social nature.
(iii) To recreate the common men.

The public panel discussions are usually organized in radio and television programmes. The current problems like educated unemployment, annual budget, increase in prices, delinking job with degrees can be discussed by a panel of invited participants.

(b) *Educational Panel Discussion* : It is used in educational institutions to provide factual and conceptual knowledge and clarification of certain theories and principles. Sometimes these are organized to find out the solution of certain problems.

The following three objectives are achieved by the educational technique :

(i) To provide factual information and conceptual knowledge.
(ii) To give awareness and of theories and principles.
(iii) To provide solution of certain problems.

Procedure of Panel Discussion

A panel discussion consists of three type of persons. It means three roles are played in organizing a panel discussion, *viz.*, panel leader, panelists and audience.

(i) *Panel Leader* : In panel discussion initial planning is necessary for the selection of panel leader. The most able and tolerant student should be selected leader. The work of a leader is to see problem and its sub-topics so that he or she may acquire a much needed overall view of the problem.

The responsibility of the leader is to direct preplanning activities to assist any member who is experiencing difficulty, and to be a liaison between the teacher and panel members. The important work of the leader is to prepare a discussion outline. This outline usually consists of a series of questions and structures around the major issues to be emphasized. The following guidelines should be of service to the panel leader:

(1) He or she is the quietest person on the panel allowing a free flow of ideas from the participats. The leader steers, judges, clarifies and summarizes in an unobtrusive manner.

(2) The leader is always mindful of his or her duties to control the remarks of the vociferous person and to encourage remarks from the more timid individuals.

(3) The leader should keep the discussion as reasonable and informative as possible. Here the leader's preplanned outline will be useful.

(4) He summarizes periodically, briefly restating the points or emphasizing areas of agreement. Whenever the leader believes it to be time to move to another point, a short summary can provide a ready transition.

(5) The leader keeps the discussion on the topic and act as a very factual person. He does not allow the participants to waver from the main theme.

(6) The leader provides smooth transitions from one aspect of the problem to another.

(7) The leader summarizes the discussion.

(8) The leader directs the question session that follows the panel presentation.

(ii) *Panelists.* The number of panelists may vary from four to ten. The members of the panel sit in semi-circle before the audience. The leader sits in the middle of the panelists. The panelists must have the mastery on the theme of the discussion so that they can exchange ideas among themselves.

Responsibilities of panel members

1. They make contribution in solution of the problem.
2. They develop inquisitive attitude.
3. The participants relate remarks to what has been said. That is essential for reaching an agreement.
4. They should be ready to consider new points of view and to alter views when warranted.

(iii) *Audience* : After the panel discussion audience are allowed to put questions and seek clarification. They can present their points of view and their experiences regarding the theme or problem. The panelists attempt to answer the questions of the audience. At the end of the discussion, leader summarises the discussion and presents his point of view. He expresses thanks to panelists and audience.

Merits of Panel Discussion

1. This technique encourages social learning.
2. The higher cognitive and affective objectives are achieved.
3. It is used to develop the ability of problem solving and logical thinking.
4. It provides the opportunity to understand nature, problem or theme of the discussion.
5. It develops interest and right type of attitudes towards the problem.
6. It develops the ability of creative thinking, the capacity to respect others' ideas and feelings and ability of tolerance.
7. It develops ability of presentation of theme and giving their points of view logically.
8. It develops the manners of putting questions and answering questions.

Limitations of Panel Discussion

The following are the limitations of this technique :

1. There are chances to deviate from theme at the time of

discussion, and the purpose of the panel discussion may not be achieved.

2. Some members dominate the discussion and do not provide the opportunities to others to participate in discussion.
3. There is possibility of the participant students spliting into two sub-groups *i.e.* for and against the theme. It does not maintain the conducive situation of learning.
4. If panelists belong to different groups, it may not create appropriate learning situation.

Suggestions for organizing panel discussion

The following suggestions should be taken into consideration to organize effective panel discussion and overcome its possible shortcomings:

1. It should be properly planned and preparation be made in advance.
2. The discussion should not be rehearsed in advance.
3. The leader should have full knowledge about the problem.
4. Sufficient preparation time should be given to the panelists. It may be one week or so.
5. The seating arrangements should be such that they can observe each other.
6. The leader should encourage every member of the panel for participation.

FIELD TRIP

When a trip is arranged by the teacher for educational communication he or she puts the school 'on wheels'. Trips take the pupils for an 'on-the-spot' study of the environment bringing them face to face with reality. Since all the experiences required for learning cannot be brought into the class-room, pupils must be taken beyond the four walls of the classroom to participate in and learn from the community. There is no better way to introduce, review, clarify and give meaning to a lesson on a process, than by a trip where the actual process can be observed. Hundreds of facts can be learned through a trip to a monument, sciences museum, Botanical garden or poultry farm. The teacher should survey the community and select such places in the locality as would be of educational value.

The purpose of field trips are to assist pupils to :

(a) Obtain first hand experiences of what they are studying and investigating.

(b) Observe and scrutinize carefully some person(s), place or activity.

(c) Get clarification of concepts and attitudes.

(d) Embark on constructional and educational activities.

(e) Broaden and change attitudes along the desirable channels.

(f) Enjoy a healthy change from the routine school setting and satisfy the urge to be out-door.

(g) Add interest, variety and involvement to learning situations.

Educational trips should be made a requirement in the curriculum. They are of three types : excursion, field trip and study tour. Excursions are planned visits to places outside the school. They are undertaken to cover short distances to see how other people live and work. The trip may be for a single or double period, a day, a week-end or a vacation. Pupils may be taken to an agriculture farm to see how the farmer works in the field, to a water supply station to see how water is purified, to house-site to see housing conditions or to a factory to observe how garments are manufactured.

Field trips may be undertaken to nearby places, often within walkable distances. Field trip does not mean that pupils should be always taken out and away from the school. The trip can be even within the school to see the garden, carpentry or S.U.P.W. workshop. It may be around the school to see the market, post office or fire station. Such trips can be completed within a single class period.

Study tours are extensive excursions involving journeys to a number of places in a sequence. A tour covers a wider area and its duration is usually longer than that for the other types of trips.

Educational trips may be independent or formal under supervision. In an *independent trip*, a group of pupils may go to a place to learn certain facts. In the *formal trips*, the entire class proceeds under the teacher's supervision to a designated places to learn specified facts.

The steps which are essential for the success of any type of educational trip are :

a. Purposing,
b. Planning,
c. Execution,
d. Evaluation, and
e. Follow-up.

(a) *Purposing* : The specific objective of organising the trip should be clearly defined and impressed upon the pupils before commencing the trips.

(b) *Planning* : Planning in advance is important in all educational trips. Planning should include :

i. Deciding the objectives of the trip and the places to be visited.
ii. Obtaining permission of the head of the institution and of the parents of the pupils concerned.
iii. Planning the detailed itinerary of all the places to be visited, with dates and timings.
iv. Collection of necessary finance.
v. Securing the written permission from the respective authorities to visit the selected places.
vi. Prior arrangement for transport and accommodation while halting.
vii. Organisation of the pupils for all the responsibilities in the trip.
viii. Collecting all the information and materials required for the trip.

The teacher and pupils must work ahead of time, set goals for the trip and plan the trip co-operatively so that the pupils are motivated, understand that the trip is educationally significant and become vitally interested in the programme planned. Before setting out they should discuss the key ideas to be observed and explored. They should pick out the specific facts to be recorded. Plans must be made for evaluating the learning gained from the trip in the light of the goals set.

(c) *Execution* : The following guidelines will be useful in the execution of the trip :

i. Prepare the itinerary and give copies to pupils and their parents.

ii. See that pupils are divided into groups. Let each group select its leader. Impress upon the pupils the need to follow the leader and adhere to the programme. Allocate specific responsibilities to the different groups, distributing all the duties to be carried out.

iii. Have a first aid box containing simple but effective remedies for common ailments such as fevers, colds, stomach aches, indigestions, headaches, bruises and small injuries.

iv. Help pupils observe decorum while visiting people and institutions.

v. Help pupils respect the prevailing customs and traditions in the places they visit, particularly the villages and tribal areas.

vi. Have all talks during the trip centred round what pupils have seen and what they will be seeing.

vii. 'Early to bed and early to rise' should be the motto during the trips to conserve strength.

viii. Help pupils listen carefully to what the guides say at different places by visit.

ix. Impress upon the pupils that they have freedom to see and explore within the limits laid by the party and hosts. The success of the trip depends upon a harmonious blending of authority and understanding.

(d) *Evaluation* : An educational trip will be incomplete, in so far its educational purpose is concerned, if it is not evaluated in terms of the purposes set prior to the commencement of the trip. Evaluation should be with reference to the understandings and appreciations of the pupils in regard to what they have seen and received at the different places visited. Check-lists and anecdotes could be used for such evaluation.

(e) *Follow-up* : The teacher must provide pupils full opportunity to discuss the trip after it is over. The conclusions based on their observations must be recorded in the reports on the trip.

Creative projects such as the following could be carried out as follow-up :

i. Writing 'Thank you' letters to all who had helped in the different places including guides.

ii. Reporting to the other classes in the school.

iii. Drawing and writing poems and stories, using bulletin boards and displays.

iv. Organising a meeting of the parents to give the highlights of the trip.

v. Organising an exhibition.

A well-planned and beautifully organised trip is education by itself, both for the teacher and the taught. It offers opportunities for work. It trains pupils to use their hands to handle their own luggage, eyes to observe keenly, ears to gather all natural information, heart to react with gratitude and love to different situations and scenes on the way and mind to assimilate all the ideas and thus stimulate the growth of the pupil in all spheres—educational, social, cultural, aesthetic, moral and spiritual.

WORKSHOP

The term workshop has been borrowed from engineering. There are usually workshops in engineering. In these workshops persons have to do some task with their hands to produce something, *e.g.* railway workshop, roadways workshop, etc. Under these workshops railway engines are repaired and manufactured. Similarly workshops are organised in education to prepare questions on the subjects in Question Bank Workshop. The participants of the workshop prepare questions of their subjects. The participants are given knowledge and training for preparing questions in the workshop.

Definition of Workshop Technique

Workshop is defined as assembled group of ten to twenty persons who share a common interest or problem. They meet together to improve their individual proficiency, to solve a problem or to externalize their knowledge and skill of a subject through intensive study, research, practice and discussion.

Purposes of the workshop

The workshop is a powerful instrument for changing and widening ideas, stimulating new ventures, developing leadership and promoting human relations and improving school programmes and procedures. It can serve several purposes, of which the important are the following :

1. During workshop the participants (members of the group) meet for exchanging ideas, establish a program of action and evaluate program success. Thus they solve education and professional problems through group process.

2. Workshop plays an important role for training in cooperation. For this personality of the leader plays a significant role. His behaviour should be good with participants.

3. Workshop stimulates creativity among participants during workshop participant are free to discuss, no work is imposed upon them and group activities are logical, sequential and integrated so they are free for thinking and creativity is a result of free thinking.

4. One of the important questions among the educationists is the one of relationship of inputs and outputs of education. The workshop gives proper thought and attention to this question *i.e.* better utilization of all available resources.

5. During workshop few persons act as a resource persons, possess superior skill and long experience as compared to participants. They bring to notice what profession literature has to say on the subject. In this way experts inspire the participants to greater heights of achievement.

Today world is rapidly changing and researches in the field of education are going on. Knowledge of innovations in education should be provided to the teacher from time to time. In this way the instructional practices as well as administrative procedures can be improved. For providing knowledge to teachers there should be some group activities where problems can be solved in cooperative manner. Thus to keep teachers up-to-date in knowledge, to refresh their attitudes and values, modern education recommends the inservice programme of containing teacher education and workshop is important means of it.

Leonard says, "Teacher participation has been an excellent means of in-service training for all. Our plan also discloses unsuspected administrative ability of a high order on the part of some teachers and broadens the horizon of them all".

Plan and procedures of the workshop

For the success of the workshop the participants should have a "felt need". Need, as psychology tells us, is a condition of the mind in imbalance or disequilibrium with the environment. If there is no "need" it is a situation of complacency, which is not conducive to action. So there must be a "felt need" and this should create a purpose. Need and purpose are different. "A feeding of need is largely an emotional matter—while concerning a purpose in largely in intellectual matter in which the situation is analyzed, means of relief are determined upon and action in accordance with such decisions is taken." The teacher of the group, whether he is the principal or supervisor, has the responsibility to stimulate the feelings, of "need" by referring to the teachers' own experiences. He is in a favourable position to do so because he is in close touch with them, he talks to them informally on many occasions. He can stimulate thinking. The teachers have had training in education and have a professional backgroud. Being a professional leader he can easily make use their technical knowledge and direct their activities and experiences.

A. **Planning**

Before starting the workshop some preplanning is essential. The planning committee should consider :

1. Duration of the Workshop including dates and venue.
2. Physical setting and resource materials.
3. Selection of participants.
4. Selection and role of resource persons.

1. *Duration, Timing and Scheduling of the Workshop* : The duration of the workshop will depend upon (a) the objectives, including nature and scope of the workshop, (b) the time availabe to the participants as well as to the organisers, and (c) others that may be perceived by the organiser.

Inasmuch as the workshop aims to improve in-service primary teacher education programmes, it should provide adequate time for review and critical assessment of these programmes and develop alternative designs for in-service education within research and evaluation.

Inasmuch as the workshop participants are key administrators representing Ministry of Education officers or units, teacher education institutions, other ministries and allied agencies, it is suggested that five to ten days be set for the workshop. The timing of the workshop is equally important and may be organised during a period feasible for the participants, *i.e.* during vocation or semestral breaks.

2. *Physical Setting and Resource Materials* : The physical arrangements including provisions for plenary sessions and small group meeting have to be examined in the light of the objectives and expected outcomes of the workshop.

A resource materials library may be set up where participants have available the national study reports, case studies reports and other relevant materials.

Funding the National Workshop—The problem of funding the workshop may be reduced to a minimum if the organisation planning committee will review it as an integral part of the total education plan, with a new dimension, research and development. It may eventually be built into the regular planning and budget process. The planning committee may also tap other resources for the workshop especially during the initial stage and the need arises.

3. *Selection of Participants* : One of the aims of the workshop is to appraise and refine previous studies, with an end in view of developing alternative designs for improving education. This implies a careful selection of participant educators, policy makers, and opinion makers who represent a broad spectrum of roles and responsibilities and can provide leadership in achieving the objectives of the workshop.

Some suggested criteria for selecting the participants include the task expectations, the social setting, and the capacity of the participants to benefit from their participation.

4, *Selection and Role of Resource Persons* : It may be advisable to invite some resource persons not only from education, but also planners, researchers, sociologists, psychologists, anthropologists, media and others. They may assist in planning the workshop and/or assist in the actual programme. The media may assist in disseminating information, stimulate public opinion and gain support for the project.

B. Communication with the participants and resource persons

After the workshop has been planned the next step is that of communication with the participants and resource persons. Pre-workshop communication with participants have been found to be valuable for workshop. Letters sent to the participants by the planning committee may include a welcome note, a clear statement of the problem objectives and programmes of activities of the workshop as well as the role of the participants before, during and after the workshop. Before communication must satisfy the following important criteria ;

(i) The problem should be within the jurisdiction of the supervisor and the teachers.
(ii) The problem should be of such a nature that the profession can help to solve it.
(iii) The problem should lead the participants to build their philosophy of education.
(iv) The problem should be of a practical nature.
(v) The problem should be such that its solution can be clearly expressed in precise language in the form of a report for future reference.

C. Contact

On first day when leader resource persons and participants meet, the leader welcomes all participants and resource persons. Leader states the problem in clear and precise manner.

D. Content

After the problem has been clearly and precisely stated the group should proceed to analyse it. Every problem is made up of smaller units or sub-problems. These plans should be chalked out by the members of the group. The leader should not lecture to the groups nor suggest his own line of action. He should neither impose his thinking on the group nor let his authority or prestige suppress their ideas and actions. His duty is to suggest readings, further discussion and exploration and try to secure a responsible consensus. Even if he finds the group differing from his own ideas and suggestions he should go along with the group and let experimentation decide the right or wrong of the course of action which the group has decided the plan should be kept flexible. If necessary, the group should modify its original plans in the light of experiences gained. Here again, the group members should be continuously involved in making changes. Leadership is best exercised when it is shared with the other members of the group. It is better of leader assign work related to sub-problems. The work groups meet as often as necessary for the selection of material, exchange of ideas and findings of individual members, who think and work together both in informal and formal manner. They should prepare reports on their respective work and present these to the whole group. So there should be session for the work group as well as general sessions for the entire group. It will be ideal to have maximum participation by all participants during the workshop. Group discussion, panel discussion, problem diagnosis and evaluation analysis of case studies and project when session for the work entire group there should be pooled. Coherent and feasible solutions of the problem should be pointed out. It is always better to have a number of alternative solutions out of which members are left free to choose and implement. The leader has the special responsibility of coordinating the efforts and findings of the sub-groups so that there is closely knit and integrated results.

E. **Evaluation**

The activities of the workshop should be jointly evaluated by the participants, of course, under the guidance of the leader. Evaluation may also be done by a committee of experienced persons, say a panel of select members of various work groups. It must be remembered that evaluation has to be made of the processes and ways of working together and of the product of the workshop but never of the members. Criteria of evaluation should be carefully drawn up.

CONFERENCE

In the area of teaching-learning in the higher classes the conference is one of the most important techniques. It is used to create higher learning situations by using appropriate instructional technique. The higher cognitive and affective objectives of education are achieved by employing the conference technique.

Conference is a technique of effective supervision. Conference may either be at the individual level between the supervisor and the teacher, or at the group level among a number of persons facing a problem about the teaching-learning situation. It is a formal because it is planned and informal because the interaction between the participants is friendly. Conferences will be profitable if the members of the group have a good relationship among themselves, cooperation, coordination and group work.

Like workshop, conferences aim at improvement of group relations, harmonious living, mutual respect and professional growth among the participants. If these conferences are to be used most profitably, the relationship between the individuals who compose the group of various groups in each school must be improved. The main difference between the workshp and conference is that a conference consists of twenty participants to thousands participants in one meeting while workshop consists of twenty or less than twenty participants.

So all that we have said about workshop, its objectives and procedures, also applies to conferences.

Conditions for Conferences

To make the conference worthwhile and effective some important conditions have to be fulfilled. These are :

1. *Consciousness of the problem* : The participants must be fully aware of the purpose of the conference and should have sufficient information about the problem. Participation in conference without adequate information about the problem and without conviction in its importance "results in the development of negative feeling and insecurity". Problem should be important to the whole staff.

2. *Recognition of the worth of each participant's contribution* : The success of the conference very much depends upon the sincere mutual understanding among the participants. In conference each participant should have unique contribution to make it working toward its solution.

3. *Organisational climate of the conference* : The physical and social environment of the conference are very important for its success. The following points must be borne in mind in order to provide adequate organisational climate:

(i) It should be held at suitable place where seating arrangements can be made according to the size of the participating group, where surroundings are pleasant and where the papers and other materials needed for the discussion are easily available.

(ii) The relationship between the participants should be

healthy, informal and well established. It is important for teachers to feel that the conference is held for solving problems and not for criticising.

(iii) The leader should not impose himself on the group. His leadership should be exercised in listening to others and inspiring them to exercise leadership by making contributions for solving the problems to the maximum.

(iv) The time of the conference is also an important factor for its success. The time should be such that the participants are fresh and full of energy.

(v) The duration of the conference should not be very long. About an hour or two are sufficient for a sitting.

4. Continuous evaluation of the progress made towards the solution of the problem and the professional growth of the participants is essential. The conference should be judged by the extent to which it succeeds in increasing the effectiveness of the teachers and promoting a better understanding among the members of the group.

Limitations of Conference

A conference technique suffers from the following limitations—

1. It is hard to predict attendance. Advance arrangements must be made for conference facilities and housing accommodation.
2. Generally the nature of topic is broad, hence discussion is confined to the specific issues.
3. Group discussion is generally dominated by the good speakers or those who talk too much and do not give opportunities to others to take part in the discussion.
4. An evaluation of the conference outcome is often difficult.

Advantages of Conference

Many advantages are claimed for the conference. Among the most significant advantages are the following :

1. Democratic tradition and values are developed among the participants.
2. A topic of common interest is discussed in the meeting of the conference.
3. It increases the interest and faith in the meeting of the confer ence.

4. It develops the habit of independent study and to think independently on a theme.

5. Ability of problem solving is developed among the participants.

6. Capacity of tolerance of ideas of others is also developed in spite of disagreements.

7. Ability of expressing ideas and feelings is developed by attending a conference.

8. Good manner for asking questions, seeking classification, presenting own point of view and defending other's ideas are developed.

TEAM TEACHING

Team teaching is one of the organizations for improving the instructional programmes. It is structured on the needs of the students, the ability of the teachers and the facilities available in an institution. Hence it is worth trying out in India. The need for reorganising the typical school programme arises out of the following factors :

1. The individual needs of a pupil are not met by completely isolating him in one room with one teacher for his total programme.
2. Intellectual development is limited by heterogeneous grouping for the entire curriculum.
3. To be grouped according to intelligence for an entire day limits academic growth in some areas and the pupils social development as well.

The team teachers are concerned with better grouping practices, curriculum revision, improved instructional techniques and more efficient use of time, energy and talents.

Historical Background

Team teaching a pattern of school organization, emerged in American education since 1954, has rapidly assumed the dimensions of a major educational movement. Starting with a few pilot projects in 1956 and 1957, the movement has now spread to several hundred communities distributed widely throughout the country. Harvard University was the first institution which initiated an internship plan in 1955. In the plan five apprentices served simultaneously under an experienced teacher for multiple relationships with adults. The second landmark in team teaching is the project in Lexington (1957-64) which was influenced by insights gained in the Harvard programme.

Francis Chase of the University of Chicago, strongly advocated the need of team teaching to use the best teachers more wisely. Emphasising the utility of team teaching he said, "Such an arrangement would allow for maximum use of the available talent, provide guidance for young and inexperienced teachers."

Team teaching developed at a high speed in seventies. All institutions use team teaching in one or the other way. Now team teaching has earned a place for itself in a number of schools and colleges both in U.S.A. and the U.K. In India, many educationists seem to be aware of this system, but they hesitate to implement it even though it will best suit to our conditions.

What is Team Teaching

Team teaching is a comprehensive term. It is a term with many faces. The sphere of team teaching is very wide. It is not limited to any one level of education. In the most general and most widely applied sense, it means giving two or more teachers joint responsibility for education of a group of pupils larger than what is generally considered a normal size class.

Shaplin has defined team teaching in these words : "Team teaching is a type of instructional organisation, involving teaching personnel and the students assigned to them, in which two or more teachers are given responsibility, working together for all or a significant part of the instruction of some group of students."

According to M.B. Naik: "In a team teaching method two or more teachers make a plan of the subject or subjects co-operatively, carry it out and always evaluate its effect on the students periodically."

This is actually a very simple version of team teaching. Team teaching is a technique of teaching the students in a collective form which makes teaching more effective and a joint venture.

Michael J. Apter has aptly remarked: "Team teaching involves bringing together a number of classes whose teaching is then the joint responsibility of the teachers of these classes who now constitute a team."

In brief, team teaching refers to the following factors or components :

1. It involves more than one teacher, *i.e.*, there is a group of teachers.
2. Teaching becomes a joint responsibility. This includes instructional planning and other aspects of teaching. Team teaching is essentially co-operative teaching.
3. It is an organation of instructional material or courses of studies at all educational levels such as elementary, secondary or college levels.
4. The number of teachers depends upon nature and objectives of the course, the size of the class and the fecilities to be used.

Objectives of Team Teaching

Any instructional strategy is developed with certain objectives into consideration. The team teaching has been developed with the following objectives in view :

1. To utilise the better talents and interests of teachers. We know that the teaching team constitutes more than one teacher who benefit the students by their special talents in the field of knowledge.
2. To increase grouping and scheduling flexibility in the grouping of children according to their interest and aptitudes in the subject.
3. To improve the quality of instruction. As in team teaching two or more experts of the subject cooperate in teaching a particular subject. Thus they help in improving the quality of instruction.

Guiding Principles in Team Teaching

Kenneth has described the following guiding principles in team-teaching :

1. *The size and composition of the group must be appropriate to its purpose* ; The size and composition of the

group for team teaching should be appropriate in terms of learning experiences and purposes of the group. The size of the group may vary according to the purpose or the goal of team teaching. The concept of fixed size class is becoming obsolete.

2. *The time allotted to any group must be appropriate to the activities of the group* : Time should be allotted keeping into consideration the importance of the subject. In team teaching arrangement a fairly fluid time table is essential.
3. *The learning environment must be appropriate to the activities of the group* : Learning environment should be provided by making arranagement of laboratory, good library, workshops, listening and viewing rooms.
4. *The duties assigned to teachers must be appropriate to their special qualification and interests* : Team teaching requires proper distribution of duties to the members of the team. The duties should be assigned on the basis of interest, qualification and personality characteristics of the individual member. Selection of members of team should be made very carefully.
5. *The level and style of instruction must be appropriate to each learner in the group* : The level of team teaching must be appropriate to each learner within the group. The initial behaviour of the teacher learners should be properly assessed.
6. *The nature and extent of the supervision of the group activities* depends upon the purpose of the groups.

Factors Responsible for the Success of Team Teaching

Following factors are responsible for the success of team teaching :

(i) Co-operation between team teachers.
(ii) Co-operation of the head of the institution.
(iii) Availability of suitable material and equipment, including rooms and audio-visual aids.
(iv) Teachers' willingness and faith in team teaching.
(v) Proper planning.

Difference between Team and Small Group

Klaus and Glasar attempt to distinguish the team from the small group as follows—

Team on the one hand, is usually well organised, highly structured and has relatively formal operating procedures as exemplified by a cricket team, on aircraft crew, or a ship control team. Team generally :

(a) is relatively rigid in structure, organization and communication;

(b) has well defined positions or member assignments so that the participation in a given task by each individual can be anticipated to a given extent;

(c) depends on the cooperative or coordinated participation of several specialised individuals whose activities contain little overlap and who must each perform his task at some minimum level of proficiency;

(d) is often involved with equipment or tasks requiring perceptual motor activities;

(e) can be given specific guidance on job performance, based on a task analysis of the teams equipment, mission or situation.

The small group generally—

(a) has an indefinite or loose structure organization and communication network;

(b) has assumed rather than designated positions or assignments so that each individual's contribution to the accomplishment of the task is largely dependent on his own personal characteristics;

(c) depends mainly on the quality of dependent, individual contributions and can frequently function well even when one or several members are not contributing at all;

(d) is often involved with complex decision-making activities;

(e) cannot be given much specific guidance beforehand since the quality and quantity of participation by individual members is not known.

Planning Process

Outline of planning process as given by Joseph C. Graunis is given below :

1. Reading of general topic of the proposed unit by teachers.
2. Survey of the written materials and other resources.
3. Teachers individually, and then together, consider scope of generalization relating to unit which is divided into phases.
4. Teachers together take out key lessons for collective planning.
5. Construction of team learning and evaluation exercises.
6. Periodic meeting for collective planning.
7. Daily planning on a contingency basis.
8. Co-ordination of team's daily plans.
9. Leaders help teachers set up conditions in classroom to facilitate planful behaviour of both teachers and pupils.

The Organization and Administration of Team Teaching

The organization and administration of team teaching involves a huge machinery and hence needs efficient personnel, mutual co-operation, proper planning and organization.

The understanding and the enthusiasm of the teaching staff are the key to success for any venture of this kind. One must get the co-operation of all teachers and staff members, see that they develop a common philosophy and access to common knowledge. Again, take time to get all parental understanding and consent, move slowly, and evaluate every move.

In the course of organisation we may encounter certain structural problems such as the size and the type of team to be organised, the extent to which all teachers are likely to become involved and the ways the proposed structure will influence the professional behaviour and the morals of participants.

Kenneth has suggested the following ways of organising teams in the process of team teaching :

1. At the secondary stage the simplest arrangement is for a number of specialist teachers to join forces in a single subject throughout the school.

2. Another arrangement is for the specialist teachers to join forces but to restrict their efforts to a particular age-group.
3. An inter-disciplinary approach may be attempted, *i.e.*, with subject specialists from different fields working together with a mixed age and ability-group.

It is necessary to provide a congenial atmosphere of work, co-operation, team spirit and fellow feelings. Every one has to be convinced that the purpose of team teaching is to bring qualitative improvement in instruction with zeal and missionary spirit. This will smoothen the problem of administration and organisation.

Team in Action

The team will be comprised of persons with different talents and, therefore, with different responsibilities. It includes team leader, the senior teachers and the team teachers. As a human organisation the team is subject to a great many stresses and strains.

a. *Team Leader*—The success of team largely depends on the quality of the team leader. He has to create general climate and provide direction and stimulation to all the team members. Actually, the person with the most authority and responsibility is the team leader. His job is to administer, co-ordinate and supervise the work and activities of the teachers and students.

b. *Competent Team Teachers*—Team teacher must be competent. The performance of the team leader greatly determines the success of the team. Performance by the leader below an acceptable standard can make the effort futile.

A team may be composed of different people with different social backgrounds. The team members' respect each other's common problems will tend to bind the team members together. A team must learn how to avoid wasting of time and how to focus its energies on the problems most deserving a full team attention.

For the effective functioning of team teaching the following factors need special consideration :

1. Combining the sections for particular subjects.

2. Meeting of team teachers, discussion and sharing of common experience.
3. Having larger groups of the students to make a selection.
4. Having groups of the students on the basis of their ability.

Team teaching is a co-operative enterprise. It is, therefore, very essential to emphasise the need for co-operative planning and teaching. Every teacher must do his work considering it as a part of team work or group work or collective responsibility. When one teacher is teaching the other may take care of classroom situations, still the other may display the aids and some one may help in maintaining discipline.

Advantages of Team Teaching

1. *Opportunity for free discussion*—Team teaching gives an opportunity for free expression to all the students of the team. Team teaching stimulates thought and discussion among teachers also who are jointly responsible for a group of children. Professional behaviour is likely to develop best where there is a strong sense of involvement and responsibility.

2. *Development of human relations*—Our present system of education does not provide enough opportunity to develop human relations among the students. Team teaching provides this opportunity and trains the students in human relations essential for social adjustment.

3. *Development of the professional status of the teacher*—Team teaching develops habit of studying new professional literature. Teachers work hard for the development of their professional proficiency.

4. *Exposure of group to more specialists*—One of the advantages of team teaching which has been recognised as an important contribution of team teaching is that students get the opportunity of exposure to more than one specialist. Thus students get opportunities to be benefited by the special knowledge of various teachers constituting the team.

5. *Break-through from a rigidly compartmentalised school organisation*—Team teaching makes more flexible use of staff, equipment and the school building. It is inspired by the determination to get rid of the traditional method of fixed time table.

6. *Economy*—Team teaching is economical method of teaching. Time and energy are saved by team teaching in maintaining discipline in the class.

7. *Evaluation*—The teachers can evaluate the teaching of one another and can give suggestions to improve it. In ordinary day to day class teaching when teachers are responsible for the work of a single class, they see little of their fellow teachers' work, nor do they have the experience of having their own teaching observed by others.

Team teaching brings them together in a group that enables them to become more aware of teaching style, more aware of their own approach and more disposed to examine alternative approaches.

8. *Quality of Instruction*—Team teaching improves the quality of instruction because more than one teacher impart knowledge relating to same subject.

Limitations of Team Teaching

1. *Lack of cooperation*—Team teaching is based on mutual cooperation among the members of the team which cannot be always taken for granted. Teachers hesitate to cooperate for the organisation of successful team teaching.

2. *Team teaching necessitates delegation of power and responsibilities*—It is not feasible in practice in our schools because the administrators do not want to delegate their powers to others.

3. *Disregard to the dynamics of small group*—One of the greatest weaknesses of team teaching today has been its disregard of the dynamics of small groups. The staff of a school does not function quite the same way as do the members of a football team. Much specific guidance cannot be given in team teaching arrangement.

4. *Traditional conservative attitude*—Generally speaking our teachers do not want to deviate from the routine methods prevalent from centuries. They resist any innovation which may bring new responsibilities. They fail to adopt themselves to the new situations and find it more troublesome.

5. *Lack of accommodation*—Team teaching needs big rooms to conduct teaching. We do not have big rooms in our schools. But as and when new teachnologies of instruction become accepted into standard practice the inadequacy will gradually

disappear. As for example, television studio illustrates the kind of development which is gradually taking place less obviously but no less surely in the schools. Even the simplest television programme is not the work of one man. It is the outcome of cooperative efforts involving a producer, teacher and technician.

6. *High cost*—Studies conducted in other countries reveal that the per student cost of team teaching is sometimes higher than the per student cost of conventional teaching.

PROJECT METHOD

One of the important principle of psychology—'learning by doing'—can be achieved by project method. Dr. Kilpatrick defines a project as "a whole-hearted purposeful activity, proceeding in a social environment". According to Stevenson, "A project is a problematic act carried to completion in its natural setting." Ballard states that project is a bit of real life that has been imported into the school". A project is thus related to real life, its problems and their solutions in social environment.

The project method is one of the modern child-centred methods. It claims that children should always have a clear idea of what they do and why they do certain things. Children's independent thinking can only be possible when they have some interest in the subject they are about to study. This interest depends on two things :

1. Whether the subject is closely connected with the child's daily life and his needs.
2. Whether the pupil realises that by learning the subject he will be able to achieve some object or purpose according to his wishes. The strong desire to achieve provides intensive stimulus and increases the interest of the student in what he does.

Characteristics of Project Method

1. It is activity oriented and students get an opportunity of learning by activity, seeing and doing.
2. The activity is purposeful and complete in itself.
3. It is aimed at problem solving.

4. It is done by students in its real or natural setting with an attainable goal.
5. It is undertaken by the students to plan and direct their learning experiences.
6. In project method the teacher encourages and help the students in learning if needed.

Types of Projects

There are four types of projects (Kilpatrick) :

1. *The producer's type*—In the producer's type of projects the emphasis is on actual production or constructions of material, object or article.

2. *The consumer's type*—The consumer's type of project consists of various experiences, such as reading and listening.

3. *The problem type*—The problem type of project aims at solving problems involving the intellectual processes of the pupils. For example to find out various pollutants in water.

4. *The drill type*—The drill type of project is directed towards attaining skills in activities such as learning vocabulary.

Steps in Developing a Project

There are four major steps in developing a project :

1. *Providing a situation*—A situation should be provided to the student by the teacher. He should discuss these situations with the pupils in order to discover their interests and to find out what things they would like to do. By way of discussion he will motivate and call the pupil's attention to the situation and leave them to the problems involved. He will explain the interest and value of the problem and the desirability of solving them. The situations are preferably from the interesting topics which are satisfying to the individual pupil. The most important point on the part of the teacher is to extend more opportunity to the pupils to express their own ideas and to have discussions among themselves as well as with the teacher at the initial stage. In this way the teacher will have simply to utilise and create a suitable situation to draw the attention of the students and observe their attitude to solve the problems.

2. *Choosing the topic*—The teacher should encourage the pupils to make their own choice of the subject for the project. In most of the cases, generally the teacher becomes tempted to

choose the project himself and tries to make the class accept his choice ; but there is very little educational value in allowing the pupils to merely accept the teacher's choice. The aim of the project method is to teach the pupils to think for themselves and to have the ability to select and choose and to carry out the purpose which they have selected. Once the pupils feels that the topic and the choice is their own, they will be interested and able to plan and carry out their own chosen project. The pupils must do their work in their own way, and the teacher merely helps them to carry out successfully what they have planned. After many situations have been provided for the pupils and many topics of interest have been discussed, the children naturally find that certain topics are of more interest to them than others. They may jot down these topics in which they are more interested and which arouse their curiosity most. More discussion follows and the teacher stimulates further discussion by means of which certain topics and suggestions can be ruled out very easily. The project must satisfy some real need of the pupils, something they really like to do. The purpose must be common to the whole class and must be acceptable to all. Then only the students participation in the learning activity is complete. Sometimes the pupils may choose unwisely, which is likely to prove a future. Here the teacher has to guide them very tactfully and manipulate the situation carefully so that the project chosen will have the most educative value and be for the good of all.

3. *Planning.* The pupil should plan the project themselves under the guidance of the teacher. The teacher will encourage all the pupils to take part in the planning by giving different constructive suggestions and will draw the attention of the pupils to the difficulties which they are likely to face. Planning may be initiated by debate and discussion. It may be followed by different proposals made by the pupils. For datailed and well thought out planning, sufficient time and much consideration is needed. The teacher has to remain alert to help the pupils in preparing the plan properly.

4. *Executing.* The fourth step is the execution of the project. Before the pupils are allowed to do the work, it is necessary that the teachers should help them to divide it into proper parts and to distributes these parts among pupils according to the plan. The distribution should depend upon the individual interest and

abilities of the different pupils in the class. In order to speed up the progress it often so happens that the teacher gives too much help, but this is a violation of the principle of project teaching in which pupils are to learn to do through actual doing. This step being the largest step in the project requires a great deal of patience on the part of the teacher and effort on the part of the pupils. In this step the pupils learn how to do a lot of activities such as going through different literatures in connection with the topic, getting down the points, oral discussion among themselves as well as with other people for the sake of obtaining different points of view and information, visiting different places of importance if and when necessary, collecting specimens of different things, studying the cost prices and selling prices, recent trends in home craft and home management and many other varieties of topic. Thus, the project method affords a great many varieties of learning for the sake of execution of the particular project selected by the pupils. It also guides the pupils to the right source of obtaining information by directing them to different places, different books and journals and helping them to get in touch with the right people who know what they really wish to learn. Guidance and encouragement are given by the teacher at every step. He reminds them constantly of the aim they have in view and helps to make changes that are necessary in the plan of the project.

Evaluating the Project. It is an important stage in project teaching which should not be forgotten. The pupils review their work and try to find out what mistakes they have made in planning or in carrying out their purpose. The pupils, thus, clear to criticise their own work and the self criticism is a very valuable form of training. The teacher's work in this evaluation is to act like a judge. A complete record of all the work done by the pupils should be written by them in their project book. This should contain their original plan. Their discussions, the allotment of work, the names of the different types of work undertaken should be entered in it and a final criticism of their own work also be written at the end.

Role of the Teacher

1. The teacher should be friend, guide and partner.
2. The teacher should provide occasions for weak students. So they can contribute something for project work.

3. The teacher should accept ideas of students.
4. The teacher should aim at inculcating scientific attitude.
5. He/she should provide democratic atmosphere in the class so that the pupils can express themselves fully without any fear of the teacher.
6. He/she should pay attention all the time to see that project is running in its right lines.
7. He/she should have thorough knowledge of each and every student of class so as to allot them work accordingly.
8. He/she should be well experienced.

Criteria of a Good Project

1. Project should be useful and practicable to the daily life.
2. Activities of project must be completed, knowledge must be gained and lead to further acquisition of knowledge.
3. Project should be interesting so that students can be active both physically and mentally.
4. There should be freedom for students to work of their own accord.
5. Project should be selected by students according to their choice.
6. It should be economical and purposeful.
7. It should be according to age interest and abilities of students.
8. Project should neither be too simple and easy nor too long and difficult.
9. Project should be according to facilities provided by school.
10. In project facts and experiences should be integrated rather than taught independently.

Merits

1. This method is based upon the laws of learning :

(a) *Law of readiness.* The pupils are made ready to learn by creating interest, purpose and life-like situations.

(b) *Law of exercise.* By practising, we learn things. There is self-activity on the part of the students. They carry on their activity in the real life situations, the experiences gained thus are very useful in the later life of the children.

(c) *Law of effect*. The sense of success and satisfaction should accompany the learning process. We usually do not false any regard of the students' inclination and feeling that is why he feels relieved and free when he leaves the classroom. This law makes it essential for the teacher to make the child satisfied and feel happy in what he is learning.

2. It develops tolerance, self-dependence, resourcefulness and other socially desirable habits.
3. It is a democratic way of learning; the children choose, plan and execute the project themselves.
4. In this method pupils develop taste for all types of work.
5. It helps the students to organise their knowledge.
6. It helps in development of creative thinking.
7. It develops habit of observation.
8. It emphasises educational content.

Limitations

1. This method is very time consuming, with the result that quantity of knowledge suffers.
2. It fails when teacher is inexperienced.
3. Syllabus cannot be covered in the limited time by this method.
4. This method is not useful for lower classes like primary and upper primary.
5. Textbooks and material written on these lines are not available.
6. It is expensive. Well-equipped library and laboratory are required for it.

Application and Suggestions

This method can become one of the good methods of teaching if a few modifications and additions are made as are suggested below. There are some misconceptions and charges levelled by teachers against this method which must be removed ;

1. Some teachers think that this method is intended to give training in modern-making only. They forget that the

main principle of the method is the purposeful enquiry and the expericnces of children in doing or achieving a certain task are practicable to their daily life as they are selected by pupils carried on in real life-situations.

2. No doubt the textbooks and materials written on the lines of project method are not available but the real project is carried out in its natural setting and so local material should be made use of.
3. The problem of expenditure can be easily solved undertaking some such project in which we can earn something or in other words the project should be made economically self-sufficient.
4. The charge of disorganised and irregular study can be removed by making a provision in the time table for formal class teaching of subjects. The first half of the day may be provided in the time table for teaching the common essential subjects and the other half for carrying out the project. This will also help the teaching in giving drill and practice in subjects like arithmetic, science and spellings etc. In this way there will be proper development of the subject and a sound fundamental knowledge of facts and principles essential for further study can be imparted.

So all the problems of insufficient, superficial and disorganised knowledge will be solved if provision is made for the ordinary class teaching also.

INQUIRY OR DISCOVERY APPROACH

Inquiry technique, as the word implies, relates to the inquiry about the topic. In this method the student is an active learner. He subjects every information or fact to ruthlees inquiry in order to know the fact for himself and to test its validity. He puts to prove the theories proposed by his teachers. Leonard S. Kenworthy, has stated—

"Two major approaches are possible in all teaching. One is the oratory approach, in which the teacher is the main actor. Lecturing and recitation on textbook content are the major methods. The major approach is through inquiry, discovery or problem solving. In it the students are the main actors. Probing, discovering, thinking, analyzing, inquiring, and solving problems are the main methods . . . ."

What is Discovery ?

The prominent workers in the field of science education advocate the use of discovery method/inquiry approach in science teaching. Many strongly favour the use of problem solving method. Webster's American Dictionary interprets discovery as: 'to discover means to know, to find out, to uncover it', etc., and discovery means anything discovered. Similarly, to inquire means 'to seek information' and inquiry means 'an investigation or examination', etc. Others describe discovery/inquiry as an attitude, a state of mind; a way of learning; a process of investigation; and a search for truth. There seems to be subtle difference between discovery approach and inquiry method. On problem solving of course, David P. Ausubel contends that it involves discovery, learning, if problem solving is meaningful and worthwhile.

The aforesaid meanings of discovery/inquiry appear to be skin deep and peripherial. A critical analysis of few definitions along with some examples will clarify it futher.

On inquiry Schwab states : "To teach Science as inquiry means, first, to show students how knowledge arises from the interpretation of data. It means, second, to show students that the interpretation of data—indeed, even the search for data—proceeds on the basis of concepts and assumptions that change as our knowledge grows. It means, third, to show students that because these principles and concepts change, knowledge changes too."

Gagne states that inquiry is apparently a set of activities characterized by a problem-solving approach in which each newly encountered phenomenon becomes a challenge for thinking.

Burner says "I do not restrict discovery to the act of finding something that before was unknown to mankind, but rather include all forms of obtaining knowledge for oneself by the use of one's mind . . . . permitting the student to put things together for himself, to be his own discovery."

Discovery-Oriented Activities

Now, we will examine two discovery-oriented activities, which are :

1. Classification of objects.
2. Interdependence of plants and animals.

1. *Classification of Objects*—Students of primary classes were given a few seeds of different colour, shape and size. The students were asked to classify them into different groups. Children observed things critically and tried to find out differences in physical properties. Many times, children changed an object in order to observe further mintutely, sometimes used instruments or aids to find out details. They repeated observation to improve reliability. Thus, on the basis of observation they perceived similarities and differences in these objects, separating them in different groups, develop arbitrary classification scheme, etc. While trying to recognize them, children were using the process of science and simultaneously gaining scientific knowledge or concepts of science. At higher grade level students may classify animals and plants and may use their own criteria of classifying things.

2. *Interdependence of Plants and Animals*—Study of an aquarium will help in understanding the relationship of aquatic plants with fishes. Children learn about the living conditions of plants and animals. They try to find out the significance of water temperature, acidity and alkalinity for living. Here, students use observational skills, classificational abilities, abilities of conducting experimentation and drawing inferences from recorded data. To acquire the concept of 'habitat' students use different modes of inquiry.

A few *characteristics* of discovery learning are discernible from the above mentioned definitions and examples :

1. Children participate actively in the process of learning.
2. Children try to learn themselves and in due course of time they become self learners.
3. Children try to organize and systematize their findings which provide an opportunity for analytical thinking.
4. The role of the teacher is minimized. But he is not out

from the teaching learning process. He functions more as a 'manager' or 'organizer' of learning activities rather than a disseminator of information.

Role of the Teacher

In this method the teacher does not give ready-made notes. He does not dominate the stage and lecture to the students. He becomes a spectator and a guide. He becomes a prompter to guide his students from the wing instead of coming to the forefront. He motivates and pricks the curiosity of the students and then goes into the background. Even then his role is very important in the following ways :

(i) He should make available all the responsive environments.

(ii) He should provide opportunity for developing further skills.

(iii) He should guide the learners at the different stages of solving problem.

(iv) The teacher should see that the learner does not become a parasite upon him. The students should not treat the teacher as ready-reckoner.

(v) The teacher should allow the students to undergo various somersaults and to hit and get hit during the process of inquiry.

(vi) He should manage the material in such a way as the learners themselves get answer to their own question.

(vii) The teacher should ensure that the learners work harmoniously on common problems and exchange notes.

(viii) He should help the learners to verify their own experimental results and findings against established facts and principles.

Advantages

(i) *Teaching through inquiry method leads to unfoldment of child's mind*—Teaching through inquiry method leads to unfoldment of child's mind instead of stuffing it with dead material. Curiosity is an innate urge of human beings, whether young or old, educated or illiterate, every one has the desire to know the unknown. This urge of curiosity has been responsible for all discoveries and inventions. Newton witnessed the fruit falling down to earth instead of getting into the sky. This led him to the famous law of gravitation.

(ii) *Inquiry Teaching has a supplementary character*—Inquiry technique supplements the existing set of knowledge by throwing open flood-gates of knowledge to be picked in both hands by the students. The knowledge gained in this way is much more superior and everlasting than that got through the sermons of the teacher.

(iii) *Inquiry technique supplies impetus to work with double zeal*—The students feel themselves in extraordinary high spirit with the topic. They take lessons just like play.

(iv) *Inquiry technique blesses the students with extra energy to face new challenges*—This technique blesses the students with added strength to face all the challenges and vicissitudes during the lesson and discovery with stamina, vigour and joy.

(v) *It is both rewarding and gratifying*—It is only through this way of teaching that ever developing subjects (particularly like science) can be judiciously taught.

(vi) *Inquiry technique ensures sublimation of natural endowments*—Inquiry technique helps in the sublimation of natural instincts.

(vii) *Besides being responsible for growth of civilization, spirit of inquiry infuses bits of good moral values*—Inquiry technique helps to develop the spirit of co-operation, team spirit, mutual discussion, other good habits and sacred values which chisel a student into an honourable citizen.

Inquiry into Three Alternative Inquiry Methods

Investigator	*Question*	*Means*	*Method*	*Ends*
Schuman	Can pupils examine and reconstruct theories ?	1. Discrepant event introduced by teacher.	Inquiry into questions asked by pupils.	1. Expansion of pupils' question asking. 2. Reconstruction of theories.

		2. Selection and organization of data by pupil 3. New theory constructed and tested by pupil.		
Strasser	Can teachers examine and reconstruct their teaching techniques ?	1. Teachers' questions and pupils responses examined by teacher 2. Teachers questions reconstructed to meet goals for pupil behaviour.	Inquiry into consequences of questions asked by teachers.	1. Expansion of teachers' question. asking 2. Reconstruction of teaching learning-theory.
Fish	Can pupils evaluate and reconstruct their methods of evaluating and reconstructing science inquiry ?	1. Discrepancy in method introduced by teacher. 2. Criteria for judging alternative methods formulated by pupils. 3. Methods of inquiring reconstructed.	Inquiry into the method of inquiry.	1. Expansion and reconstruction of science inquiry methods. 2. Expansion and reconstructing of methods of evaluating and reconstructing science inquiry.

PROBLEM SOLVING METHOD

In the opinion of John Dewey, the world famous educationist and philosopher, education is not preparation for life but is life itself. In other words, pupils should share in the solution of different problems already confronted or yet to be confronted by them in their life. The pupils should feel that the school is a real community for them. They should utilise those creative powers and critical thoughts during their student life which will be used by them for solving their problems in their future life. So there should be close relationship between the education received at school and the real life situation, between theory and practice. Learning by doing is the gospel of Dewey's progressive education. Experimentation is the fundamental principle of his education. The application of thinking and reasoning power of each and every individual is the basic requirement of the educational system. According to Dewey, development of the critical intellectual power is one of the aims of education and this power is developed only through problem solving.

Meaning of Problem Solving

Thomes Risk has defined problem solving as a planned attack upon a difficulty or perplexity for the purpose of finding a satisfactory solution. This involves the process of reflective thinking, not merely the accumulation of facts or the blind acceptance of ideas which someone in authority gives us.

Risk has further elaborated it. He says that problem solving teaching procedure is defined as a process of raising a problem in the minds of the students in such a way as to stimulate purposeful, reflective thinking in arriving at a rational solution. In this definition three elements are involved. These are :

1. A situation which presents some difficulty or doubt which requires solution.
2. A goal or end involving some aspect of the situation for which no ready answer is given.
3. A desire or motive that stimulates an attempt to find the answer.

Ausubel has suggested that problem solving involves concept formation and discovery learning is a part of problem solving.

Characteristics of a Problem

The problem to be solved arises out of a life or an educational situation. For the application of problem solving as a method of teaching, the problem selected must be clear, definite, understandable, thought-provoking, interesting and suited to the age, needs and capability of the learners and the knowledge they already possess. It should have practical value, be capable of completion within the time limit, set without causing additional financial commitment to the problem-solver or to the institution. Above all the problem should correlate with the curriculum.

Systematic approach to problem solving involves two important types of procedures, namely, inductive and deductive.

The Inductive Procedure

The inductive procedure demands the thinking process to move from the particular to the general. General conclusions are arrived at from concrete examples and generalisations from particular principles. Science poses many problems which may be put to inductive reasoning. An example for inductive problem solving is : Vitamin C dissolve in water and is easily destroyed by heat. This leads to the generalisation that all food rich in vitamin C, should be cooked in minimum water for the least amount of time.

The Deductive Procedure

In the deductive procedure, reflective thinking moves from the general point to the particular. For example, pupils find that foods have less Vitamin C after cooking and explore the reasons for the loss. They arrive at the inference that heat and water had reduced Vitamin C. Thus the pupils have 'deduced' the particular principle from the generalised observation.

A class exercise may be turned into a problem when the problem demands an integration of the learnings entire repertory of strategies and understandings. Exercise should follow real or hypothetical problems, to sharpen skills and to reinforce the processes used in the problems.

Types of Problem : Problems differ in the purposes for which they are used : (a) developing information or a new principle (developmental problem), (b) making decisions (judgement problem); (c) making pupils think creativity (planning problem).

(a) General principles taught in the class are followed with home assignments involving their applications. Pupils develop abilities when the general principles are put to use through developmental problems.

(b) Through solving judgement problems, pupils gain judgement through experiences involving decisions.

(c) Good managerial ability results through correct planning. Planning problems should be accompanied by developmental problems through which knowledge is gained and judgement established. A problem should be expressed clearly, completely and in terms of the understanding of all the pupils of the class. The problems solving method involves the use of reflective thinking or reasoning.

Steps to be followed in using the problem solving method

The steps involved in using the problem solving method are :

1. Sensing or selecting the problem.
2. Defining the problem.
3. Formulating hypothesis.
4. Collecting relevant data.
5. Formulating the tentative solutions.
6. Arriving at final solution.
7. Testing the validity of the solution finally arrived at.

1. *Sensing or Selecting the Problem*—The pupil must feel the problem his own. He must feel its challenge to his thinking. The teacher should guide the pupils in recognising the problem to be solved, by creating suitable situations to motivate the learners. She/he should help them to alert to recognise the problem as and when they occur.

2. *Defining the Problem*—After the class has come to feel the problem as its own, the teacher must next see that it is stated in definite terms and constantly held before the pupils.

Hullfish and Smith suggest the following questions to be raised in defining the problem.

(a) Exactly what is the problem ? Can it be broken down into sub-problems ?

(b) Is there likeness of this problem with others ?

(c) What is the fundamental difference ?
(d) What does this difference entail new methods ?
(e) Should I now redefine the problem ?

3. *Formulating hypothesis* : In order to focus attention on the problem, students should identify the purposes for which the problem has been undertaken. The investigator should hypothesize the relationship between two or more variables or difference between two or more treatments. A review of previous research in this area may suggest several possible causes of this problem. These possible causes may be stated as hypothesis. These hypothesis are 'educated guesses' or possible solutions.

4. *Collecting Relevant Data* : After defining the problem to the pupils, they must be stimulated and helped to collect the relevant information which is basic to its solution. The investigator should conduct the experiment or should try to study the observations made or should gather data based on his experiment. A life science teacher should guide the students to conduct experiments with proper procedure. The teacher may suggest the source to be tapped, the books to be referred to and the person to be consulted. The information collected should be evaluated for its relevancy to the problem and applicability.

4 *Formulating the tentative solutions* : Different solutions to the same problem may be studied in depth to decide upon the most appropriate solution and procedures. The pupils cannot rush to arrive at the solution. The inferences drawn must be considered and a tentative solution formulated.

5. *Arriving at final solution* : The tentative solutions are pooled together and discussed. This phase of problem solving technique requires a great amount of guidance and coordination from the teacher, so that pupils can select the correct solutions and arrive at suitable inferences.

6. *Testing the validity of the solution finally arrived at* : The validity of the solution finally arrived at may be tested through the application of the hypothesis to new situation further experimentation and investigation and gathering new data.

The teacher needs to motivate the learners to take up problem solving challenges by creating an atmosphere conducive to fact finding, she/he should guide the pupils constructively throughout different stages of the problem solving venture.

Limitations of Problem Solving Method

The main limitation in the application of the problem-solving method is when the teacher starts to assign the problem without leading the learner to choose the problem, then the interest of the pupils is killed. Another limitation is that it is highly time consuming for both the teacher and the learner and, therefore, cannot be used frequently. Often there is paucity of sources of references for the learners if the problem solving effort taken up becomes the only mental activity, the other aspects of learning get neglected. The teacher, therefore, needs to adopt problem-solving judiciously and scientifically to bring about, development of scientific attitudes in pupils so that they will be equipped to apply scientific procedures in solving their daily problems.

Advantages of the Problem Solving Method

Many advantages are claimed for the problem solving method. Some of these are very important for they conform to the highest aims of teaching. Among the most significant advantages are the following :

1. It conforms to life. Everyone is confronted with problems all through life. Why should we not master the technique for solving problems in the school ?
2. It arouses interest and hence aids in the educative process.
3. It leads pupils to form judgements. This is of vital importance in a democracy, where the success of government rests in the final analysis with the people.
4. It makes for pupil activity. This has been the cry of educators since the opening of the century. The pupils change from passive members of a class into an active class.
5. It challenges the intellect of the pupil rather than his memory.
6. It does much to destroy the credulous belief in the printed page. In solving the problem the teacher can place different types of material before the pupil.
7. It permits the pupil to get thought from the printed page.

8. It enables the pupil to evaluate the printed page, thereby distinguishing between primary and secondary sources or between what is not.
9. It develops the traits of open-mindedness and tolerance. The pupil finds that there is more than one side to a question.

6

TESTING, MEASUREMENT AND EVALUATION

Testing, measurement and evaluation are sometimes interchangeable. Hence it often becomes a source of confusion. *Testing* means to give test to know the quality. For example in case of textiles, testing means testing the strength, whereas in case of classroom it may mean testing the individual intelligence.

Testing involves the use of some specific instruments or set of instruments to determine a certain quality or trait or a series of such quality or traits.

In education testing has come to have a rather specific and somewhat limited connotation and a slightly unfavourable process. Some persons regard a tester as a technician who is more interested in the scores and statistics of the results rather in what the results mean in relation to the boys and girls . If the pupils do not do well on a test, the test gets a bad name undeservingly since the fault usually lies in the way it was used.

Measurement is thought as having broader and more pupil-centred objectives than a testing programme. It includes a greater variety of instruments than testing. Measuring instruments include rating scales, check-lists, or score cards and many devices which can yield quantitative results. Measurement implies a broader interpretation of results than testing.

Evaluation is considered as being the broadest among testing, measurement and evaluation. Evaluation includes both qualitative as well as quantitative instruments. Evaluation programme makes use of such devices and methods as anecdoted records, observation of children without any special attempts to make such observations quantitative, children's work samples, and the like. Evaluation is dependent upon and largerly limited to qualitative judgements, descriptive accounts and opinions. Evaluative techniques are time consuming. If a teacher is to keep his records in a way that will give meaningful and fairly reliable results, a great deal of his time will be required.

The term evaluation is a simple process which without much effort or work on the part of anyone, provides answers to some of the most difficult educational problems. An evaluation procedure is useful only to the extent that it yields data which are accurate and which mean that they seem, or are believed to mean.

The evaluation has contributed materially to the development or importance of using different kinds of instruments and relating data from one to another. Evaluation has also called attention to the importance of traits or qualities or conditions not easily measured by objective tests.

Whether the process be called testing, measurement or evaluation it is not as important as it is that the progress, a status of the learner with respect to the desired goal, is being determined. Evaluation has emphasized the need for a great variety of measures or samples of an individual's behaviour and it has stressed the interrelatedness of such information in understanding and helping the individual.

Standardised Vs. Non-Standardised or Teacher-made Tests

The standardised tests and teacher-made tests differ around the purpose for which they are constructed. The standardized tests are constructed for general use. They are not prepared by a teacher to measure the achievement of a child in the subject matter which has been taught. Their application is made in general to make a comparative study between one school and another and between one class and another.

Anastasi considers that a psychological test is essentially an objective standardised measure of sample behaviour. Standardization means uniformity of procedure in administering and scoring the test.

Cronbach states : "A standardized test is one in which the procedure apparatus and scoring have been fixed so that precisely the same test can be given at different times and at different places."

The Standardised Test has following characteristics :

(i) *Norm*—It means normal or average performance.

(ii) *Objectivity*—A fully objective test is that in which each examiner reaches the same conclusions regarding the evaluation of an individual.

(iii) *Reliability*—A test is reliable when there is consistency in the scores of an individual at different occasions.

(iv) *Validity*—The validity of an examination depends upon the efficiency with which it measures that it attempts to measure.

(v) *Usability*—By this is meant the degree to which the test or other instruments can be successfully employed by classroom teachers and school administrators without an undue expenditure of time and energy.

Teacher-made Tests

The standardised tests are more pure as compared with the teacher-made tests. The teacher-made tests are constructed by the teacher to evaluate the achievements of their pupils. The teacher-made tests may be broadly classified into essay and objective types. The fullest benefit occurs to the student from the use of both.

Reliability

A test can be fully reliable when there is consistency in its results on it being administered at different occasions. Anastasi is of the view that "the reliability of a test refers to the consistency of score obtained by the same individuals on different occasions or with different sets of equivalent items." In short, we can say that reliability means consistency. It is not necessary that if the test has reliability, it will be valid as well.

The reliability is measured through reliability co-efficient. The reliability coefficient is obtained by giving the two equivalent forms of the same test to the same subject at two different times, using the same techniques and whatever scores are obtained in both the tests their correlation is obtained. This correlation is known as reliability coefficient. We can measure the reliability,

Methods of Determining Reliability

There are four procedures in common use for computing the reliability coefficient of a test. These are :

1. Test-retest (repetition)
2. Alternate or parallel forms
3. Split-half technique
4. Rational equivalence.

1. *Test-retest* (*Repetition*) *Method*—Repetition of a test is the simplest method of determining agreement between two sets of scores : the test is given and repeated on the same group, and the correlation computed between the first and second set of scores. Although test retest is sometimes the only available procedure, the method is open to several serious objections. If the test is repeated immediately, many subjects will recall their first answers and spend their time on new material, thus tending to increase their scores. Besides immediate memory effects, practice and the confidence induced by familiarity with the material will almost certainly affect scores when the test is taken for a second time. Moreover, transfer effects are likely to be different from person to person, if the net effect of transfer is to make for closer agreement between scores achieved on the two givings of the test than would otherwise be the case, the reliability coefficient will be too high. On the other hand long (*e.g.* six months or more) interval and if the subjects are young children, growth changes will affect the retest score. In general growth increases initial score by various amounts and tends to lower the reliability coefficient.

Given sufficient time interval between the first and second administration of a test to offset in part at least, memory, practice and other carry-over effects, the retest coefficient becomes a close estimate of the stability of the test scores. In fact, when the test is given and repeated, the reliability coefficient is primarily a stability coefficient.

The test-retest method will estimate less accurately the reliability of a test which contains novel features and is highly susceptible to practice them it will estimate the reliability of test scores which involve familiar and well learned operations little affected by practice. Owing to difficulties in controlling conditions which influence scores on retest, the test-retest method is generally less useful than are the other methods.

2. *Alternate or parallel forms method*—When alternate or parallel forms of a test can be constructed, the correlation between Form A, for example, and Form B may be taken as a measure of the self-correlation of the test under their conditions, the reliability coefficient becomes an index of the equivalence of the two forms of the test. Parallel forms are usually available for standard psychological and educational achievement tests.

The alternate forms method is satisfactory when sufficient time has intervened between the administration of the two forms to weaken or eliminate memory and practice effects. When form B of a test follows Form A closely, scores on the second form of the test will often be increased because of familiarity. If such increases are approximately constant (*e.g.* 3 to 5 points), the reliability coefficient of the test will not be affected, since the paired A and B scores maintain the same relative positions in the two distributions. If the mean increase due to practice is known, a constant may be subtracted from Form B scores to render them comparable to those of Form A.

In drawing up alternate test forms, care must be exercised to match test materials for constent, difficulty and form ; and precautions must be taken not have to the items into two forms too similar. When alternate forms are virtually identical, reliability is too high ; whereas when parallel forms are not sufficiently alike, reliability will be too low. For well made standard tests, the parallel forms method is usually the most satisfactory way of determining reliability. If possible, an interval of at least two to four weeks should be allowed between administration of the test.

3. *The Split-Half Method*—In the split-half method, the test is first divided into two equivalent halves and the correlation found for these half-tests. From the reliability of the half test, the self-correlation of the whole test is then estimated by the Spearman-Brown prophecy formula as given below :

$$r_{II} \frac{2r_{\frac{1}{2}\frac{I}{II}}}{1+r_{\frac{1}{2}\frac{I}{II}}}$$

Where r_{II}=reliability coefficient of the whole test

$r \frac{1}{2} \frac{I}{II}$=reliability coefficient of the half-test, found experimentally.

The split-half method is employed when it is not feasible to construct parallel forms of the test nor advisable to repeat the test itself. The split-half method is regarded by many as the best of the methods for measuring test reliability. One of its main advantages is the fact that all data for computing reliability are obtained upon one occasion, so that variations brought about by differences between the two testing situations are eliminated.

A marked disadvantage of the split-half technique lies in the fact that chance errors may affect scores on the two halves of the test in the same way, thus tending to make the reliability coefficient too high. This follows because the test is administered only once. The longer the test the less the probability, that effects of temporary and variable disturbances will be cumulative in one direction, and the more accurate the estimate of score reliability.

Objection has been raised to the split-half method on the grounds that a test can be divided into two parts in a number of ways, so that the reliability coefficient is not a unique value. This criticism is true only when items are all of equal difficulty ; or when, as in personality inventories ; items may take any order. It is true also, of course, in speed tests. In most standard tests items are arranged in order of difficulty so that the split into order and events provided a unique determination of the reliability coefficient.

4. *The Method of "Rational Equivalent"*—The method of rational equivalence, represents an attempt to get an estimate of the reliability of a test, free from the objections raised against the method outlined above. Two forms of a test are defined as "equivalent" when corresponding items, a, A, b, B, etc., are interchangeable ; and when the inter-item correlations are the same for both forms. The method of rational equivalence stresses the inter-correlations of the items in the test and the correlations of the items with the test as a whole. Richardson and Kuder formula for determining test reliability has been used which is given below :

$$r_{II} = \frac{n}{(n-1)} \times \frac{\sigma 2 + \Sigma pq}{2t}$$

r_{II}=reliability coefficient of the whole test

n=number of items in the test

σ+=the SD of the test scores.

p=the proportion of the group answering a test item correctly.

q=(l−p)=the proportion of the group answering a test item incorrectly.

Validity

Before a test can be used, it is necessary to make certain that the intended interpretation of the test score is justifiable. The process of gathering evidence to determine what a test score means to called validation. By means of such research, the test developer or user determines how well the proposed interpretation accounts for scores on the test. The more fully and confidently a test can be interpreted, the greater is its validity.

Any given test may be used in many ways and may be given interpretations. An arithmetic test may be used to predict success in high school science, to help assign marks in a course, or to analyze a student's performance and point out his particular weaknesses. Each use calls for a somewhat different interpretation and leads to a different type of decision. The test might be highly satisfactory for one purpose and quite inadequate for the other. It is, therefore, necessary to validate a test with reference to each particular purpose for which it is to be used. A test can be considered valid only when it is used with those students who have intellectual ability and background of experiences comparable to it. By this, we mean that a test which is constructed for ninth and tenth classes will be unfit for sixth or seventh classes. In this way, validity is a specific trip of any test. It is incorrect to ask "Is this test valid ?". Since any test is valid for certain purpose and not for others.

Here one more thing is to remember that any test will be valid only when it is reliable. If any test has zero validity then it will not be correlated with any other test.

Types of validity : There are various types of validity. The following are in common use ;

1. *Concurrent Validity*—It is similar to predictive validity in some respects. It differs mainly in regard to the time when the assessment test is given. In establishing predictive validity, the predictor test is given first and the assessment test at a later date. An example of concurrent validity is the correlation between scores on a test purporting to measure anxiety (the predictor variable). Administration of the test of anxiety and assessment by the psychiatrists both take place at approximately the same time or concurrently. Hence the term concurrent validity. Concurrent validity can also be established by correlating scores on the test that is to be validated with scores on a second test, purporting to measure the same traits, for which validity, particularly predictive validity, has already been established. Scores on new intelligence tests, for example, are often correlated with scores for the same subjects on the Stanford-Binet test.

2. *Construct Validity*—In this validity, the test is judged in terms of a particular construct, or theory, about the relation between the test scores and other significant variables.

Sometimes a test cannot be justified on the basis that it is clearly related to a particular assessment measure. For example, given a test purporting to measure intelligence, with what assessment of intelligence should it be correlated to demonstrate its validity ? Should it be correlated with grades in school ? It seems reasonable to assume that grades are related to intelligence, but there are other factors in intelligence beyond the ability to get good grader-possibly leadership ability for example, or critical thinking, or creativity.

Similarly, it might be hypothesized that a test of creativity could be considered valid if high scores were obtained by those who have many hobbies and interests, are singled out by their teachers and associates as being creative, and behave and think in unconventional ways.

The evidence gathered provides reason to believe that the function of the test is consistent with a given theory or psychological construct, of creativity. This kind of validity is called construct validity.

3. *Content Validity*—When authorities agree that the question on a test afford adequate coverage of a subject, the test is said to have content validity. Classroom achievement tests are ordinarily best judged on the basis of content validity. The teachers who are

specialist in a particular subject may examine a test and determine whether it covers the desired content areas.

4. *Face Validity and Content Validity*—Face validity means that on the surface the items in a test appear to be valid. This appearance of validity may, however, be misleading, the test may in fact be measuring something different from what it appears to be measuring. For example, a test purporting to measure degree of anxiety might contain such a question as "Do you believe that you are an exceptionally nervous person ?" On the surface, this might seem to be a good question for helping identify people who are anxious. The more anxious person might be expected to say, "Yes, I am more nervous than the average." Suppose, however, that anxious persons tend to deny that they are more nervous than the average. If this is the case, then even if the question has face validity it would not have content validity. For a test to have content validity, it should be demonstrated through detailed analysis of test content that the items are a valid measure of the subject or behaviour to be assessed. Face validity—the surface appearance of validity—is not enough.

Objectivity

The objectivity is a necessary trait. A fully objective test is that in which all the examiners reach the same conclusion regarding the evaluation. In the definition of a psychological test by Anastasi, the word 'Objectivity' has also been used. In this definition, objectivity means that this test is independent of the individual judgement of an examiner. The tests are considered objective only to that extent to which they are independent of individual judgement in examining a subject, in measuring his scores and interpreting them. In short, we can say that in an objective test whosoever be the examiner, the individual will obtain the same scores. This is, however, very difficult to achieve in the practice because, till now no such instruments of standardization and objectivity have been framed which can make a test fully objective.

PROJECTIVE TEHNIQUES

L.K. Frank was the first person to use the term Projective Techniques in 1939. Ruth Strang says : Projective Techniques are a method of understanding the inner world of the individual. According to Murray, the purpose of this project is to stimulate literary activity. It is based on the fact that when a person interprets social situation he is apt to expose his own personality, his characteristics, ideas, attitudes, aspirations, fears, worries and the like—projective techniques are very useful with young children, illiterate persons with speech defects or language handicaps.

Kinds of Projective Techniques

Play Situation : In this technique the thoughts, impulses and feelings of a child are revealed through games or toys. Situation is such as to give free play to his ideas at the unconscious level. Like if some dolls are given to a boy, who is afraid of his father, might assign no doll to his father and the like.

Story telling and Story Completion : Here an incomplete story may be given to a child and he be asked to complete it. A child will surely reveal something about his feelings and desires while completing it, like if some emotional incident is given to a child to complete it when a child completes such stories he depicts his innermost feelings, wishes and thoughts. This method is mostly employed in the case of delinquent children.

Incomplete Sentence Technique : Through this simple method, the Psychologist gets clues of child's repressed wishes, complexes, likes and dislikes, his positive and conflicting attitudes.

Original Drawings and Paintings : This method provides vital information about the child's personality. The theme or subject he chooses the colour, length direction, curvature of the lines or any prominent figures give indication of the various traits of his personality.

Dream Analysis : It has been said that dreams have their roots in person's private world. Therefore, this dream analysis reveals out the repressed, unconscious desires or emotions of individuals.

Free Association : Here in this method the psychologist encourages the person to talk freely and develops a rapport with him. In doing so he records the individual's responses and later on interprets them.

The Rorschach Test : Rorschach was a Swiss Psychologist who employed this method of ink blots for diagnosing mental disorders. The ink blots which are not well defined figures are perceived by each individual in his own way, thus projecting his own personality. This method is used for various purposes :

(1) To distinguish between normal persons and persons in need of psychiatric treatment.

(2) Shows the potential intelligence of an individual.

(3) Helpful in indicating personality characteristics significant for vocational success.

Thematric Apperception Test (T.A.T.) : This method of Murray'sinvolves pictures of dramatic events. The individual observes and identifies with some pictures. To quote Ruth Strang, he reads into the pictures his own experiences and the responses made in the test situation reveal the person's attitudes and ways of thinking.

Main Points of TAT Pictures

(1) No detail in the background so that it may not limit to a certain time or place.

(2) Themes of these pictures are vague.

(3) Expressions of characters in pictures are rather vague.

(4) The contents do not convey the whole story.

(5) Situations relate to the ordinary situations of life.

(6) The child can easily identify himself with the characters of pictures.

Advantages of Projective Techniques

1. An individual reveals himself on unconscious level in various situations.
2. We get reliable information.
3. Prompt spontaneous responses are elicited.

Limitations

1. They are apt to give very subjective results.
2. They are very difficult to interpret for an average student of psychology.

3. Only psychologist can administer them properly.
4. Projective techniques are often time consuming.
5. Few projective techniques are standardised.

INTEREST INVENTORY

In an interest inventory, the interests of one individual are compared with the interests of those individuals, who are successful in any profession, or industry. From the comparison we are able to find out the vocation in which an individual's interests lie and so he can give proper vocational guidance. For example, if the interests of an individual compare favourably and have a high correlation with the interests of successful scientists, we can safely advise him to take to scientific research as his profession.

In an ordinary sense interest inventories are not tests. We do not mark the answer of the questions put in them as right or wrong. Through them we only try to assess the interests of the individual.

Bighm says that there are four reasons why we should try to find out the vocational interests of an individual. It is because of his interests that (i) we can find out whether the individual will remain satisfied in performing the special type of activites; (ii) we are able to know whether that individual has the same interest which the others in that profession have, in other words, we can find out if he is capable of having good relations with other employees, (iii) we can predict that a man can get more success in those activites in which he is interested, however, it is to be remembered that a high interest in one subject does not always indicate a high success in that subject; and (iv) we can direct his attention towards those activities about which he has never thought, that is, he may be asked to adopt that profession for which he may not have applied his mind in the ordinary course of event.

The interest inventories in which use are : Strong's Vocational Interest Blank, Cleeton's Vocation Interest Inventory, and Thurston's Vocational Interest Schedule. In India many interest inventories have been developed. Most of them are on the lines of the interest inventories which have been developed in other countries.

ATTITUDE SCALES

Attitude is the degree of feeling favourableness or unfavourableness towards some object, person, group, institution, idea of proposition. Different types of scales have been evolved to measure attitude, but Likert's and Thurstone's Scales are the most common.

Likert Scale (Method of Summated ratings) : About 50 to 60 statements clearly expressing favourable or unfavourable opinion towards the target *i.e.* the issue towards which the attitude is to be measured are collected, from literature or essays written by a sample of the population whose attitude is to be measured or are in the last resort written by the investigator himself. Half of the statements should be favourable and half unfavourable. The statements are arranged at random and a five point rating scale, containining the points 'strongly agree', 'uncertain', 'disagree' and 'strongly diagree', is set against each. The list is printed or cyclostyled and circulated in a sample of about 200 members of the population concerned and the members are required to respond to each statement by indicating on the rating scale as to how far they agree or disagree with the statement. The statements should fulfil the following :

(1) They should be short, straightforward and unambiguous; rarely more than 20 words.

(2) They should be intelligible to the population of which the attitude is to be measured.

(3) They should not state a fact, instead of expressing an opinion, with which all have to agree or disagree, for example, 'students have to study for the examinations' or 'students do not need to study for the examinations'.

After the respondents have finished with the list, the items are evaluated for selection in the final draft in the following manner.

The scripts are scored by awarding 0, 1, 2, 3, 4 and marks for strongly diagree, uncertain, agree and strongly agree responses respectively in case of statements expressing a favourable opinion and in the reverse direction in case of unfavourable statements. The awards in each statement are totalled for each script and the scripts are arranged from top to bottom in the descending order of the total marks, and then top 25% to 27% of the scripts and the same percentage of bottom scripts are taken out. After that the mean scores of each item in the top and bottom piles are computed and the significance of their difference is tested with the help of the following formula :

$$t = \frac{Mt - Mb}{\sqrt{\left(\frac{Vt}{NT} + \frac{Vb}{Nb}\right)}}$$

where Mt = Mean top
Mb = Mean bottom
Vt = Variance top
Vb = Variance bottom
NT = Number of top scripts
Nb = Number of bottom scripts

Wherever the 't' value is +1.65 or more the difference is considered significant (since one-tailed test is applicable here) and the item suitable for selection. All such items are arranged in descending order of numerical value and 10 to 15 top favourable and the same number of top unfavourable items are selected for the final draft 20 to 30 items. These items are randomly arranged in the final draft which is administered and scored in the same manner as the preliminary one.

Thurstone Scale (Method of Equal Appearing Interval) : Here too about 60 statements are collected in the same manner as for the Likert scale and they are also required to have the same qualities as enlisted under that scale, but there is one more requirement for the statements for the preliminary drafts of the Thurstone scale. They should express all shades of attitude from strongly favourable to strongly unfavourable, inclusive of some neutral statements about 5 or 6. After they have been collected and edited they are written on separate slips of paper without any rating scale against them and about 30 judges are asked to put each of them in one of the eleven or nine categories starting from most unfavourable to most favourable, supposed to be as equal intervals, according to nature of the attitude expressed by it. Now it has been proved that no difference will ensure if the statements are not separated and the judges are asked to express the category they think each belongs to by placing the numerical 1 to 9 or 11 against it.

If we prefer the nine point scale '1' would mean most unfavourable, and 9 the most favourable, with neutral 5 in the middle. Thus the numbers would be said to have the following meanings :

1. Extremely unfavourable
2. Very unfavourable
3. Unfavourable
4. A little unfavourable
5. Neutral
6. A little favourable
7. Favourable
8. Very favourable
9. Extremely favourable.

After the judges have categorized the statements, a frequency table of each statement is made separately showing the number of the judges which has put it in each of the different categories from 1 to 9. From this the cumulative frequencies and proportions are computed and the Q_1, Q_2 and Q_3 values are found out graphically or by mathematical computation. The Q_2 value of each statement is its scale value, that is, its position on the scale continuum starting from O and ending at 9. The value $Q_3 - Q_1$ is the ambiguity value which should not exceed 2. About 20 to 30 statements are chosen on the following two criteria :

(a) The Q value of none of the chosen statements should exceed 2, and the less the better.
(b) The scale values of the selected statement should be almost evenly spread all over the scale.

It may be noted that the scale value of a statement is the category value below and above which half the number of judges place it. The Q value is the category range between which the opinion of the middle 50% of the judges spread and the higher this value the greater the difference of opinion among them. Hence, the less this value the more preferable the statement is.

Administration and scoring—After the statements have been selected they are arranged in a random order and administered to the people whose attitude is to be measured. There are no rating scales against the statements. The respondents are asked to tick mark those statements with which they agree and leave the rest. The mean or the medians of the scale values of the statements tieked by them is their score.

Reliability and Validity of the Scales—For reliability of both Likert and Thurstone scales, two parallel forms may be prepared and administered one after the other in quick succession and the scores on the two correlated. For validity of both the scales, two contrasted groups already known for their strongly favourable and unfavourable attitudes towards the issue under study are taken and their attitude measured with the constructed scale and if the difference between the mean score comes out to be significant the validity of the scale may be accepted.

Comparison of the two scales—The Likert scale does not have any known scale range and the scores on it do not indicate the positions of the respondents on the attitude scale with reference to the neutral point, as in the Thurstone scale. Hence, it is useless for pinpointing the attitude of an individual because the score will not tell whether his attitude is neutal or how much away from it on the favourable or unfavourable side. Of course, for other purposes, that is, for comparing the attitude of persons or groups and for making correlational studies it is as effective as the Thurstone Scale.

OBSERVATIONAL TECHNIQUES

Rating Scale

Rating is a judgment technique, particularly where opinions are to be collected regarding people. The supervisors are asked to pool their opinions through selecting a number on a scale which indicates a degree of given characteristics. The teachers are required to rate their students with respect to certain attributes. The ratings are then entered on a cumulative record, for current and future use. Rating is a convenient way of pooling opinions, rather than relying on meetings and discussions between the evaluators.

The nature of rating scales used influences their effectiveness. The breadth of category to be rated is a major determiner of the effectiveness of rating. If a person is asked to rate personality he will be faced with a far different task than if he is required to rate more limited characteristics such as honesty, attitude toward others, attitude toward authority, appropriateness of dress, appearance and speech. One may be asked to rate academic effort in general or some specific aspect of it, such as study habits, class attitude, punctuality and attention. An overall rating may be asked for after a number of judgements on narrower categories have been made but ratings on more limited and better defined characteristics are more effective.

A rating scale is most meaningful if a sufficient number of steps are included usually from five to ten steps. As few as three steps limit the rate to high medium and low. As many as fifteen steps are confusing, and the middle steps represent such slight degrees of difference as to be meaningless. The steps of a good scale are not too diversified and each characteristic is accompanied by verbal descriptions suggestive of each level in the scale. A scale of one, two, three, four and five judging conduct is not as good as a scale which reads : 1. Poor ; 2. Fair ; 3. Good; 4. Very Good, 5. Excellent.

More descriptive material can be included, but often does not enhance the definitiveness of the scale, and may confuse the choices. It is best to make the word description as full as possible without sacrificing the clarity of carefully chosen one word descriptions.

The ability to judge people is based on appropriate norms, chiefly arising from the similarity of background of the judge and the subject. This ability is based on general and social intelligence on an intuitive judging factor and especially on motivation (a strong desire to make accurate judgement). Improvement in the ability to judge follows from the opportunity both to voice one's prejudices and feelings, and to consider one's contribution objectively so that doing leads to development.

In actual measurement of the traits by rating scale many types of errors are committed. One such error is the generosity error. This means that the raters are liable to put their acquaintance on the more desirable side of the average. In this respect, some raters may be more generous than others. But this error can be correct by statistical means provided the same rater rates a large number of individuals.

A second error which can also be committed is known as the 'halo effect'. If an individual creates a favourable impression by excellence in one trait one is more inclined to rate him near the top in every other trait without further discrimination. Similarly, if the subject has created a bad impression at one time the rater finds it quite difficult to stake off the impression when he is rating him in various other traits.

The Individual Interview

The most fruitful device for evaluation is the individual interview. It is friendly, private, and the person being evaluated need not be made to feel if the interviewer is skilful. It is expensive in terms of time, and it is valid and reliable only according to the skill of the interviewer. The personal adjustment of the individual at the time is also a factor which disturbs validity and reliability but this may be compensated for through the use of several interviews. Rating and test scores supported by interviews provide for the most adequate evaluation of an individual.

In interviewing the interviewer must safeguard against premature judgement. He should not form his notions on the basis of first impressions which are often misleading. Before finalizing his opinion he must give the subject a good chance to reveal himself. One defect in this technique is that it is subjective and hence unreliable.

Observation

The device of data collection is used by the researcher when he observes some specified behaviour of the subjects, *e.g.*, the aggression of children. This tool has certain advantages and disadvantages, which are the following.

Advantages

1. Personality is better assessed by observation of overt behaviour than by self-reporting which may hide facts.

2. The behaviour can be observed in natural setting and hence the interferences can have applicability to ordinary life situations. This is called 'external validity' *i.e.* applicability beyond the observed situation.

3. The tool does not need any communication medium, hence it can be used for collecting data regarding infants and

illiterates or people who do not understand the observer's language.

Disadvantages

1. The covert behaviour and traits cannot be observed.

2. Though the interferences have applicability to ordinary life-situation, yet the internal validity of the inferences may be low in uncontrolled situations (natural setting without any experimental controls) as the data collected may not be reliable and valid. The observations may get coloured by the subjectivity of feelings of the observer and suffer in reliability. Their validity may be low because they may be due to some uncontrolled interfering variable not relevant to the study.

3. It is time-consuming and needs highly trained observers.

4. The behaviour of grown up people becomes artificial when they become conscious of the observer.

Types of Observation

The mode of observation may be classified in the following ways. Each has one or the other of the advantages and disadvantages enumerated above.

1. *Uncontrolled observation*—The observation is made in an ordinary natural setting. It has all the advantages and disadvantages discussed earlier.

2. *Controlled observation*—The behaviour is specified and well defined. If it is a behaviour trait like 'aggression'. Its symptoms are identified and observed in standardized situations, in standardized periods of time and in standardised and well defined units in order to increase the internal validity but the 'external validity' may suffer as the standardized situation is not there in life outside. Of course, standardisation of the techniques of observation would not affect it, and is desirable even for uncontrolled observation in order to impart some internal validity to it. An example of standardised technique of recording observation of teaching is Flander's interaction analysis of verbal behaviour.

3. *Camouflaged observation*—Here the situation and the units of measurement are both standardised but what is being observed is kept a secret from subjects. On the other hand, they are made to believe that they are being observed for something else and

that way do not become conscious regarding the observed behaviour, *e.g.*, for selections of officers in the army the candidates may be made to act, to show their powers in a standardized situation while actually they may be observed and assessed for some other traits like 'cooperation', with well standardized instruments.

Observation is classifiable along one another dimension too, besides the degree of control, namely, regarding the role of the observer in the activity. Thus it is categorized as non-participant observation and participant observation.

1. *Non-paricipant observation* : The observer keeps aloof and observes the subjects as they act. This facilitates proper and immediate recording of the incidents but it makes the subjects conscious and distorts their behaviour. Of course, these days observers may use tape-records and video tapes for recording facts even in their absence. They may replay these gadgets later on and record the observation for analysis. It may be pointed out that non-participant observation does not affect small children for long. They become a little conscious at the beginning but then they foregt the adult and go on in their natural way. This is the way, observation technique is mostly used in researches pertaining to infants and nursery children.

2. *Participant observation* : Here the observer himself participates with the subjects in the activity. This establishes proper rapport. There is no distortion in behaviour. But the recording of the observations becomes a problem. It cannot be done simultaneously and later on forgetting ensues. Moreover, it is not possible to participate in the activities if there is a big age gap between the observer and the participants, as is likely to be in case of educational researches pertaining to adolescent students.

ANECDOTAL RECORD

A Systematic procedure for gathering observational data, a method used more frequently and informally is the anecdotal record. This is the teacher's written record of an occurrence or incident involving a child. It is not easy to know what is significant and worth recording. Teachers have preferences and dislikes about their pupils, often without being fully aware of them, and these biases tend to influence the choice of children about whom anecdotes are recorded, as well as the nature of the anecdotes. It is quite natural, also to overlook the shy, quiet child and to record ancecdotes only on the more aggressive children.

A recurring question on the matter of anecdotal records concerns the number of children on whom to keep such records and the number of anecdotes to record. Some authorities advocate that anecdotes be regularly recorded for all children. Ideally this is certainly desirable but in most situations it would be impractical for busy teachers. It should be noted that keeping anecdotal records presents quite different problems for elementary and high school teachers. Records of anecdotes should be made as soon as possible after the incident has been observed, but never so that pupils are aware that this is being done. Many teachers find it best to make a few notes at the first opportunity and then to make a complete record during free time at noon or after school. Anecdotes should always be recorded on the same day if this is at all possible, for the longer the time elapsed between the occurrence and the recording of it, the less distinct and accurate one's menory of the incidents becomes. Anecdotes are probably best recorded on cards. Each anecdote may be recorded on a single small card, or, as is sometimes preferred, several anecdotes may be recorded on one large card. Cards are the most convenient means of record keeping since they are easy to file, sort, handle and arrange.

SOCIOMETRY

It is a device for obtaining a picture of the social interaction, speciality in the classroom which is the main setting for educational researchers.

For this the students are asked to name one or more classmates with whom they would like to associate in some particular activity, *e.g.* studies, games, excursion, etc., and on basis of their responses a 'sociogram' is drawn on a plain paper. For each student is represented by a circle and from each circle arrows are drawn to those other circles with whom he would like to associate. Where the choices are mutual the arrows have head at both the ends. From the sociogram 'stars' and 'isolates' can be identified. 'Stars' may be defined as those whom more than 50% of the group like to associate with and the 'isolate' as those who are not chosen as associates by anybody.

Steps in preparation of sociogram

It is necessary, therefore, that a beginner in research should understand the method of preparing a sociogram. In the following example we take hypothetical data to illustrate the procedure of making a sociogram.

Example : When asked "With whom would you like to go out for a picnic" From a compact group of 10 students in a tutorial class, their responses in the form of I, II and III preferences were as below :

		A	B	C	D	E	F	G	H	I	J
	A		I		II						III
	B			I	II	III					
	C				I		II				III
	D	I	II	III							
	E			I		II	III				
	F	I			II			III			
	G	II	I			III					
	H		I	II			I				III
	I				I		II	III			
	J		I			II	III				
Total No. of	I	2	4	2	2	0	0	0	0	0	0
	II	1	1	1	3	1	2	0	0	0	0
	III	0	0	1	0	2	2	1	1	0	3

From the data, it is clear A gives I choice in favour of B, II choice in favour of D and the third choice for J. Similarly others' choices can also be located from the Table. Considering only I choice we find that B is liked by most followed by D, C and A. For preparing a sociogram B is put in the centre and D, C and A are put in the next circle. Other cases fall in the remaining concentric circles. The relationship on the basis of I choice is indicated in the following diagram.

From the figure, it my be seen that B is favoured by maximum number of students in response to the question asked. The persons placed on outmost circles are not liked by any one, as far as the first choice is concerned. But they are liked by students in their second and third choice except 'I', who is liked by none. He, in this situation will be classified, as an 'isolate'.

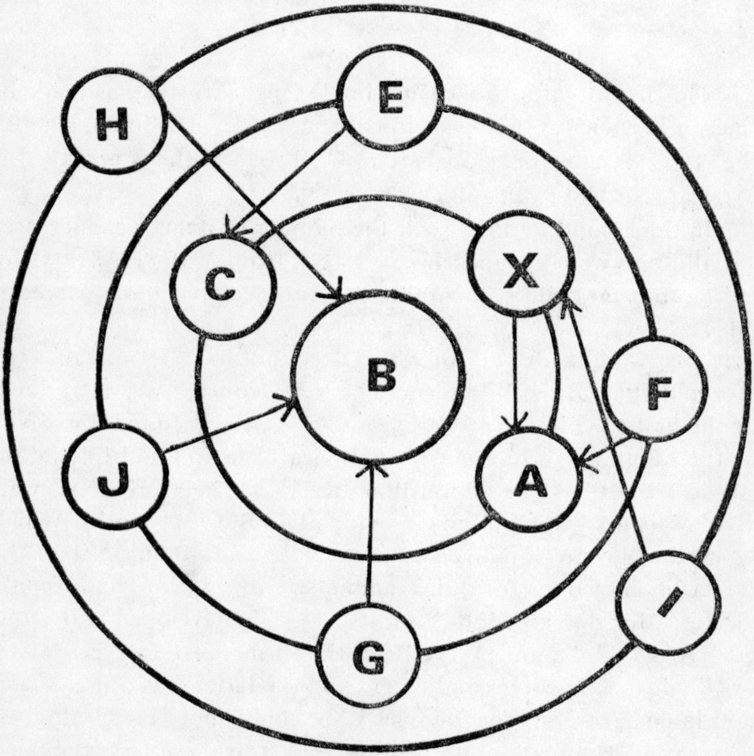

If the students are asked "with whom you would not like to go out for a picnic", the responses of students would reveal the position of a person who is neither liked nor disliked. Such a person will be placed in the category of 'rejectees'.

A number of studies of the personality traits of 'star' and 'isolates' has been made. The sociograms also reveal closed subgroups within a group or class and these are called 'cliques'. Studies of the 'cliques' have also been made in some researches.

QUESTIONNAIRE

In this tools a large number of questions are asked in writing to gather information regarding, anything, an event, a situation, an institution, a custom, or person's behaviour etc. When it is used for assessing a person's behaviour or personality it is often called an 'inventory', and when it is used in a face-to-face situation it is called a 'structured' or 'directed' interview.

INTELLIGENCE TESTS

This fist attempt to measure intelligence directly was made by Binet, a French Psychologist, in collaberation with Simon, in 1905. The 1905 Simon-Binet scale consisted of 30 items arranged in increasing order of difficulty.

In the second or 1908 scale the number of items was increased and all items were grouped in age levels, from 3 to 13 years, for finding out a child's mental age. Another revision appeared in 1911, when Simon died. In America a number of different revisions were made out of which the Stanford revisions of 1916, 1936 and 1960 are well known. The 'I.Q.' concept was introduced for the first time in the 1916 revision. The I.Q. is found by dividing the Mental Age by the Chronological Age and multiplying the Quotient by 100. The Simon-Binet tests and their revisions were all administered to children individually. But in World War I the need of group intelligence tests arose for administering them to recruit in groups for quick administration in order to make selections for different jobs. Americans then developed two group tests, Army Alpha and Army Beta, the former was a verbal test for English knowing candidates and the latter was a non-verbal (non-language) test for people who could not read English, because of being illiterate or foreigners. In these tests the items were not arranged in age level groups. The I.Q. equivalents were computed by finding out the mean score of an adult sample on the test and the Standard Deviation of the scores. The mean score was given a value of 100 I.Q. which means average intelligence and for every I.S.D., above the mean 15 I.Q.'s were added and for every I.S.D. below the Mean 15 I.Q.'s were subtracted. These are called 'Deviation' I.Q.'s.

The Army Alpha and Beta Test proved the precursors of

many group verbal and non-verbal intelligence tests. The latter are mostly pictorial test.

Examples of Group Verbal Tests of Intelligence developed in our country are the following :

1. Test were developed separately for age levels, 6, 7, 12 and 13 by Manovigyanshala, Allahabad, in Hindi. For finding out the Deviation I.Q. equivalent of the raw scores of each test, the Mean scores and the S.D.'s were found out from sample of the age level to which the particular test pertained.

2. Group Test of Intelligence in Telgu : Developed by Bureau of Educational and Vocational Guidance, Hyderabad for age leval 10-16 years.

3. Pathak Vikash in Marathi, for age range 3-13 years, developed by A.K. Pathak.

4. R.C. Das and G.N. Das test in Oriya for age group 12 to adulthood.

5. Kannada Test of Intelligence, for 14-18 years.

6. Sadharan Mansik Yogyatia Priksha (Punjabi), for 11-16 years constructed by S. Jalota and L.B. Singh.

Manovigyanshala, Allahabad, U.P. has adapted Pidgeon's Non-Verbal Test of Intelligence for the age range 10-15 years.

In the performance tests, the problems are presented in material forms and the given objects that can be moved about. The subjects are required to respond not by writing but by manipulating cubes or card or wooden pieces to make required designs or fit them in holes of different shapes.

Examples of performance tests :

(1) Seguin's Form Board Test, in which pieces of different shapes have to be fitted in corresponding holes.

(2) Koh's Block Test, in which coloured cubes have to be arranged in different designs as painted on cards.

(3) Bhatia's Performance Test Battery : it has five different tasks,

7

ELEMENTARY STATISTICS

TABULATION AND GRAPHICAL REPRESENTATION

Collection of Data

In educational research various tests are administered from time to time with a view to establishing individual difference, ascertaining relative status of students in a group, and assessing significant group trends pertinent to the specific objective of the test administration. Besides, for the purposes of research, the data based on surveys or experimental observations is made use of, for building up the scientific body of knowledge, or for solving the immediate problems. In either case, investigator or classroom teacher comes across a mass of data comprising individual scores. This mass of unordered data is known as raw data and all statistical investigations start with this type of fundamental information. Classification and description of this data is needed for interpretation and meaningful presentation. This classification leads the investigator to understand basic features of the data. A frequency distribution of data represents its arrangement in an orderly manner so as to indicate the frequency of occurrence of the different values of variable falling within arbitrarily defined intervals of the variable. Its meaning will be made clear in the present chapter alongwith its graphic representation.

CLASSIFICATION OF DATA

Interpretation of Scores :

Scores by themselves have no meaning, 55 out of 100 may be a good or a bad score depending on a variety of factors, such as the difficulty of the test, the ability of the class, and the standard of marking by the examiner. Therefore, 55 out of 100 means little; more needs to be known before it can be judged as a good, average or poor score.

We cannot interpret score of a student unless we know about the score of other students who appeared in the same examination. For example 53% may be good in one case and poor in another. Consider the scores of two sets A and B :

Set A	30,	40,	45,	50,	53,	55.
Set B	50,	60,	53,	70,	75,	80.

In set A, score 53 is above the average score and can be considered as good score but in Set B, it is below the average and, therefore, here it is poor.

Hence to judge where a score is good or bad reference must be made to the average score of the group.

Even in two sets of sources with the same average, some score may have different meaning. Consider the following two sets of scores :

Set C	15,	25,	35,	45,	55,	65,	75,	85,	95.
Set D	35,	40,	45,	50,	55,	60,	65,	70,	75.

In both the sets of scores the average of scores is 55, here the score 75 has a different meaning each. In set C, 75 is the third best score whereas in set D, it is the best score.

Thus, we observe that one must also know something about distribution of scores of the set in order to assess the value of a particular score.

Hence, the scores of two tests should not be compared unless the averages of the scores of the two tests and their distributions are similar.

Distribution of Scores :

Consider the following 40 scores of a class on an arithemetic test :

8, 6, 2, 5, 10, 9, 3, 2, 1, 6, 7, 5, 4, 5, 0,
2, 5, 6, 7, 4, 3, 4, 6, 8, 5, 7, 4, 3, 5, 3, 4, 9,
5, 7, 6, 5, 3, 1, 4, 6.

It is difficult to see from the above list how the scores are distributed. Inspection of scores, however, shows that many scores occur more than once.

We observed that there are two 9s, two 8s, four 7s and so on, This suggests that we may arrange the data in columns, as shown in Table 1. In one column we may arrange the possible scores in descending or ascending order and in the other we record by tallies (opposite to the respective marks) the number of students who scored these scores. When we have to record five tallies we mark four thus //// and the fifth is made across the four thus 𝍸. The tallies are then totalled in the next column. This column thus lists the number of times each score occurs. Such an arrangement of data is known as frequency distribution and the number of times a particular score value occurs is known as frequency of that score. The value of score is generally represented by the symbol X and its frequency by the symbol 'f'. The total number of frequencies is denoted by 'N'.

TABLE 1

Scores	*Tallies*	*Frequencies*
10	/	1
9	//	2
8	//	2
7	////	4
6	𝍸 /	6
5	𝍸 ///	8
4	𝍸 /	6
3	𝍸	5
2	///	3
1	//	2
0	/	1
Total		N=40

In table 1 the data have been classified in as many classes as there are score values within the total range of the variables. In the above example, maximum score was 10 and minimum possible score was 0. In this way we had only 11 classes. But when the range (the interval between the highest and lowest score) of scores is large, we shall have large number of classes if we classify in as many classes as there are score values.

If the classes are more than twenty in number it becomes difficult to handle them. Therefore, in such cases we reduce the number of classes by arranging the data in arbitrarily defined sub-groups. Consider the following scores of 50 college students :

85	66	76	45	66	91	77	64	71	74
47	78	76	42	70	58	71	67	80	78
73	48	68	87	81	72	65	69	73	84
75	57	58	87	56	72	62	93	73	83
97	81	51	61	53	72	62	79	88	79

Inspection of the above scores, shows that the highest score is 97 and the lowest is 42, so the range is 55 (*i.e.* 97—42). Therefore, the distribution of scores can be conveniently arranged by dividing the range of 55 into ten or more classes if the classes are taken to be of 5 points each and we take starting points 40, then the scores within the range 40 to 44, that is, all scores with the values 40, 41, 42, 43 and 44 will be grouped together to form the lowest class. All scores from 45 to 49, that is 45, 46, 47, 48 and 49 will form the next class. Similarly we shall group all scores within the ranges 50 to 54, 55 to 59, 60 to 64 and so on. The highest class will be 95-99.

The students should note that the beginning score of the lowest class was taken 40 and not 42 which was the actual lowest score.

Theoretically classes of 42 to 46, 47 to 51, 52 to 56 etc. are as good as classes of 40 to 44, 45 to 49, 50 to 54 etc. but the second set is easier to handle from the point of view of tabulation as well as computations which will come later.

TABLE 2

Class Interval	*Tallies*	*Frequencies*
95-99	/	1
90-94	/	2
85-89	////	4
80-84	𝍸 /	5
75-79	𝍸 ///	8
70-74	𝍸 𝍸	10
65-69	𝍸 /	6
60-64	////	4
55-59	////	4
50-54	//	2
45-49	///	3
40-44	/	1
		N=50

Conventions regarding the formation of classes :

In the frequency distribution as shown in the Table 1, the original observations have been retained and we can reconstruct the data from the frequency distribution without loss. When the interval is more than 1, as in the above example it is 5, some loss of information regarding individual observation is incurred. In such cases the original observations cannot be reproduced exactly from the frequency distribution.

In the class interval is large in relation to the total range or the set of observations, this loss of information may be appreciable. If the class interval is small, we shall have large number of classes and there shall be very little gain in convenience over the utilisation of the original data. Therefore, we choose such a class interval which is neither very small nor very large. The following conventions are generally used in the selection of class intervals :

(i) The class intervals should be well defined and should not overlap. 0-4, 5-9, etc. should be used in preference to 0-5, 5-10 etc.

(ii) The class intervals should be of such a size that with

such class intervals the total range of observations is covered by 10 to 20 intervals.

(iii) Start the class interval at a value which is multiple of the size of that intervals or a zero. For example, with a class interval of 5, the interval should start with the values of 05, 10, 15 etc., with a class interval of 2, the intervals should start with the values 0, 2, 4, 6 etc.

(iv) The class intervals should be of uniform size and commonly of 3, 5 or 10.

Steps in the Construction of a Frequency Distribution Table :

1. Determine the range of scores.
   Range = Highest score — Lowest score.
2. Decide on how many categories or step intervals are required. Normally, the number of intervals used is not less than 10 and not more than 20.
3. Divide the range by the number of intervals giving the actual size of each step interval. If the interval size does not work out to be a whole number, it is advisable to round it off. Usually, the class intervals are taken to be equal to 3, 5, or 10.
4. Construct the class interval column starting with the lowest score or a convenient score. Add the class interval size to this score to get the upper score of the class. Repeat this procedure until the class interval column includes an interval into which the highest score can be placed.
5. Mark a tally for each individual score against the class interval in which the score falls.
6. Total up the tallies within each class interval and place in the frequency column.

Exact Limits of the class interval

Where the variable under consideration is continuous and not discrete, we select a unit of measurement and record our observation as discrete, for example, like in statistical measurement we measure the achievement of a child and award full scores of 44 or 26 or 80 instead of fractions. It seems that the series is discrete, but though achievement is a continuous variable. When we record an observation in discrete form and the variable is a continuous one (like the one we have just quoted), we imply that the value recorded represents a value falling within certain limits, usually one-half a unit above and below the value reported. Hence, a score of 44 on a continuous variable will represent a class interval 43.5 to 44.5 (*i.e.*, all values greater than or equal to 43.5 and less than 44.5). These are called the exact limits of class interval or class boundaries or end value. Similarly, the class

70-74

69.5 ——————————————— 74.5

class interval

interval "70-74" in the previous example will include all values greater than or equal to 69.5 (the lower limit of 70) and below 74.5 (the upper limit of 74), *i.e.*, it covers all values between 69.5 and 74.5.

Cumulative Frequency Distribution :

Sometimes we are not concerned within the class intervals themselves, but rather with number of percentage of values 'greater than' or 'less than' a specified value. This can be obtained by adding successively the individual frequencies. The new frequencies obtained by adding individual frequencies of class intervals are called cumulative class frequencies. If we denote individual class frequencies of the successive class intervals by f_1, f_2, f_3 . . . . . fk the cumulative frequencies will be f_1,f_1+f_2, f_2 +f_3 and so on.

Graphic Representation of Frequency Distribution :

Graphic representation often facilitates understanding of a set of data. If the graph is well drawn, it is usually easier to read and interpret than the table. We shall consider here only those graphs which are useful in visualizing the important properties of frequency distributions. These will be of great help in enabling us to comprehend the important features of frequency distributions and in comparing one frenuency distribution with another. Four methods of graphic representation of frequency distribution are in general use :

(i) Histograms.
(ii) Frequency polygons.
(iii) Cumulative Frequency curve.
(iv) Cumulative Percentage curve or Ogive.

Before we proceed to discuss the method of representation of tabular data graphically, we would like to discuss some of the general conventions for the construction of graph and certain basic ideas in drawing of graphs.

Drawing of a graph :

Before we consider the procedure of constructing a frequency polygon or histogram, we would like to discuss with you the simple algebraic principles applicable to any graphic representation. Graphing or presentation of any distribution on a graph paper is done with reference to two lines *i.e.* coordinate axes, one, the vertical line or Y-axis, the other, the horizontal or X-axis. Usually, these two lines are taken perpendicular to each other and their point of intersection is called origin 'O'. This is the point of reference for both the axes.

Some convention for the construction of graph :

1. In a frequency distribution graph, it is customary to let the horizontal axis represent scores and the vertical axis the frequencies.

2. The arrangement of the graph should proceed from left to right. The low numbers on the horizontal scale should be on the left, and the low number on the vertical scale should be at the bottom.

3. The distance along either axis selected to serve as a unit is arbitrary and effect the appearance of the graph. Some writers suggested that the units should be selected such that the ratio of height to length should be roughly 3:5. This prodedure has some aesthetic advantages.

4. The vertical scale should be so selected that the zero point falls at the point of intersection of the axes. When data do not start with a zero it is customary to designate the point of intersection as the zero point and make a small break ff in the vertical line. Similar procedure is followed for the horizontal line.

5. Both the horizontal and vertical axes should be appropriately labelled.

6. Every graph should be assigned a descriptive title which states precisely what it is about.

7. Scale of measurement (or units selected) should always be mentioned on the graph.

Now we go to the procedure of drawing a graph.

Ex. 1. Draw a histogram of the following distribution in Table 3.

TABLE 3

Class Interval	*Exact Limits*	*Frequency (f)*
88-90	87.5-90.5	1
85-87	84.5-87.5	1
82-84	81.5-84.5	2
79-81	78.5-81.5	2
76-78	75.5-78.5	5
73-75	72.5-75.5	2
70-72	69.5-72.5	5
67-69	66.5-69.5	6
64-66	63.5-66.5	8
61-63	60.5-63.5	4
58-60	57.5-60.5	4
55-57	54.5-57.9	3
52-54	51.5-54.5	4
49-51	48.5-51.5	2
46-48	45.5-48.5	1
		N=50

Histogram :

A histogram is a graph, where the frequencies are represented by areas in the form of rectangular bars. The height of such rectangular bars is the frequency and width of such bars in the length of respective class intervals (taking into consideration, the exact lines).

Solution :

Step 1. Draw two straight lines perpendicular to each other, the vertical line near the left side of graph paper, the horizontal line near the bottom of it.

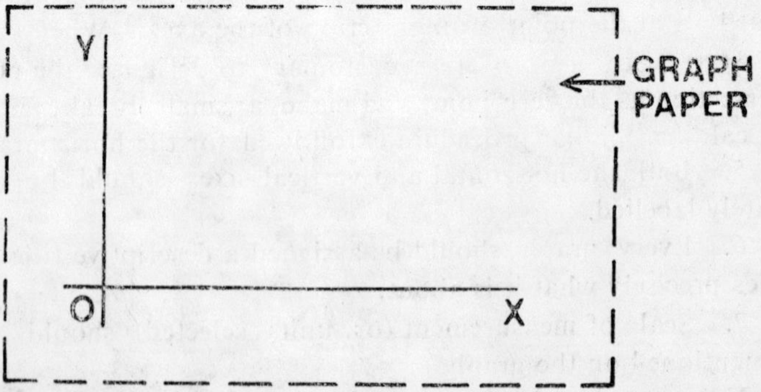

Step 2. Label the vertical line (the Y-axis) OY, and the horizontal line (the X-axis) OX. Put the O (origin) where the two lines intersect.

Step 3. Lay off the scores (or C.I.) of the frequency distribution at regular distances along the X-axis. The exact limits of the scores (or C.I.) are to be taken. Select X unit such that it will allow all the scores (or C.I.) to be represented easily on the graph.

Step 4. Mark on the Y-axis successive units to represent the frequencies of the different intervals. Choose a Y scale which will make the largest frequency (the height) of the histogram approximately 60 to 80% (or roughly 5%) of the width of the figure.

Step 5. Draw rectangles.

Note—Units are mentioned on the upper right corner of the graph.

Frequency polygon

A frequency polygon is a closed figure where the frequencies are represented by the height of the perpendiculars from the mid-points (or mid-values) of each class interval.

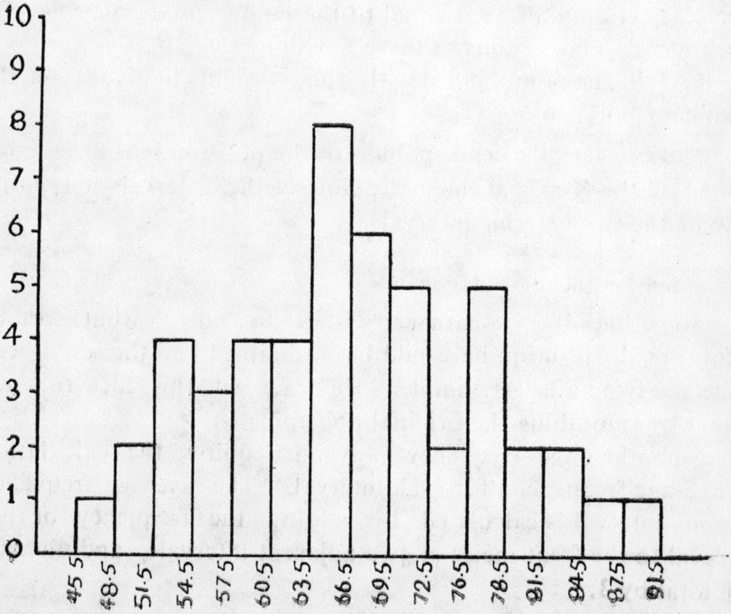

In the construction of the frequency polygon, after the usual steps in the drawing of any graph, points are plotted above the midpoints of the intervals on the X-axis. Frequencies are represented in each case by a dot. When all the points are located, they are joined by a series of short lines to form a frequency curve. In order to complete the polygon, an additional interval at the high and low ends of the distribution is included on the X-Scale. The frequencies on each of these additional intervals is naturally zero. The polygon is closed by joining the mid-points of these two extreme intervals.

Example

Represent the frequency distribution in table 3 as frequency polygon.

Solution

Follow the steps 1 to 4 given in example 1, except that in step 3, instead of taking the exact limits of scores, take the mid-points of the class intervals. These mid-points are to be marked off on the X-axis.

5. At the mid-points of each interval on the X-axis go up in the Y direction a distance equal to the number of frequencies on the interval. Place points at these locations.

6. Join the points in (5) with the straight lines to get the frequency polygon.

Notice that the end points of the polygon have been positioned on the X-axis at the mid-points of the intervals on either side of the two extreme intervals.

Smoothed Frequency Polygon

Sometimes the researcher wishes to know what sort of frequency distribution he would have obtained had the data been collected from a larger sample. He can get this idea to some extent by smoothing the original polygon.

Smoothening a frequency polygon requires the calculation of average frequencies for each interval. The average frequency for any interval is calculated by adding the frequency of that interval to the frequencies of two adjacent intervals, and dividing the total by 3.

For example in Table 4 the average frequency for the interval 49-51 is the frequency of that interval (2), added to the frequency of the interval 46-48 (1) and the frequency of the interval 52-54 (4) divided by 3.

$$\frac{2+1+4}{3}=2.3$$

This procedure is repeated for each of the class intervals. When an interval has only an adjacent interval, then missing interval is given a frequency of 0.

For example, the average frequency for the interval 80-90 is

$$\frac{0+1+1}{3}=0.66$$

Table 4 shows the frequency distribution with average frequency for each of the class interval. The smoothed frequencies are ploted for polygon. If this is superimposed over the original frequency polygon, then comparison can be made as to the shape of the curves.

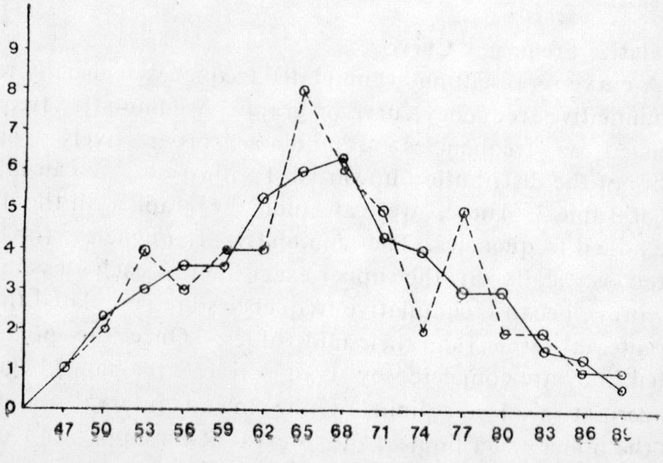

TABLE 4 : **Frequency distribution (smoothed frequencies)**

Class Interval	*Mid-points*	*f*	*Average or smoothed frequency*
88-90	89	1	0.6
85-87	86	1	1.3
82-84	83	2	1.6
79-81	80	2	3.0
76-78	77	5	3.0
73-75	74	2	4.0
70-72	71	5	4.3
67-69	68	6	6.3
64-66	65	8	6.0
61-63	62	4	5.3
58-60	59	4	3.6
55-57	56	3	3.6
52-54	53	4	3.0
49-51	50	2	2.3
46-48	47	1	1.0

Cumulative Frequency Curve

A curve representing accumulated frequency is usually termed as 'cumulative frequency curve or graph'. A cumulative frequency is defined as frequencies accumulated progressively from the bottom of the distributlon upwards. To illustrate, we can take the help of Table 3. There, we can plot the graph with the help of these added frequencies. The cumulative frequencies (or f) are plotted vertically at the upper exact limit of each class interval (or scores), because cumulative frequencies are cumulated through each interval rather than their mid-values. Once the points are plotted, they are connected by straight lines (free hand) beginning with zero at the lower limit of the lowest interval and ending with the upper exact limit of the interval at the upper end of the scale.

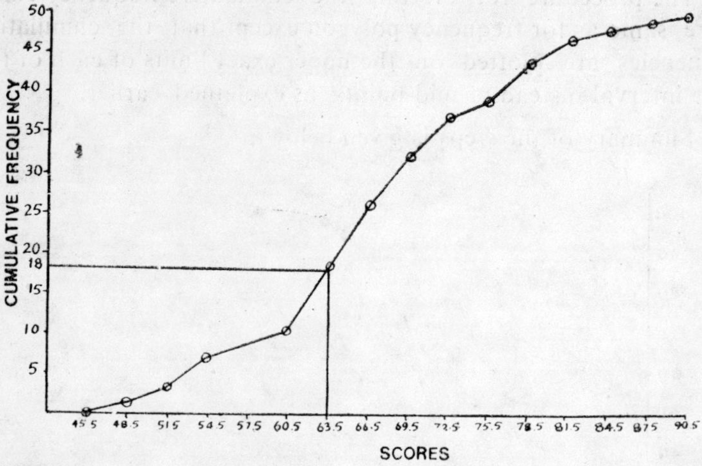

Example 5

Plot a cumulative frequency graph of the distribution given in Table 5.

TABLE 5 : **Cumulative Frequency Distribution**

Class Interval (scores)	*Class Interval (Exact Limits)*	*X*	*Cumulative Frequency (cf)*
88-90	87.5-90.5	1	50
85-87	84.5-87.5	1	49
82-84	81.5-84.5	2	48
79-81	78.5-81.5	2	46
76-78	75.5-78.5	5	44
73-75	72.5-75.5	2	39
70-72	69.5-72.5	5	37
67-69	66.5-69.5	6	32
64-66	63.5-66.5	8	26
61-63	60.5-63.5	4	18
58-60	57.5-60.5	4	10
55-57	54.5-57.5	3	14
52-54	51.5-54.5	4	7
49-51	48.5-51.5	2	3
46-48	45.5-48.5	1	1

The procedure for plotting the cumulatlve frequency curve is the same as for frequency polygon except that the cumulative frequencies are plotted on the upper exact limits of each of the class interval instead of mid-points, as explained earlier.

Summary of the steps is given below :

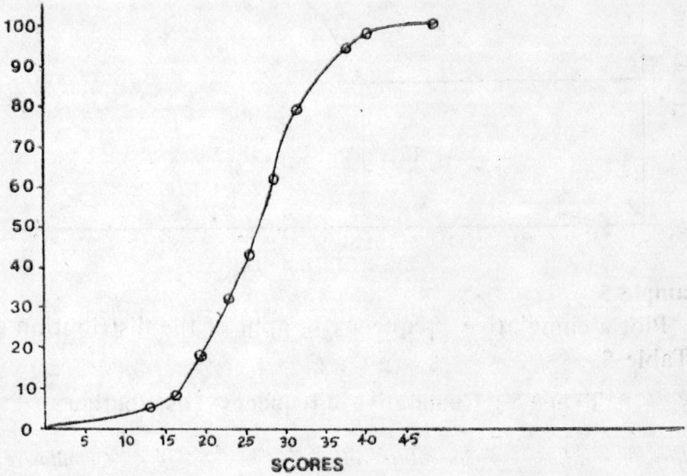

1. Draw the axes.
2. Mark off upper exact limits of each of the class interval on X-axis and cumulative frequencies on the Y-axis, by selecting appropriate units.
3. Plot cumulative frequencies for each class interval on the upper exact limit of the interval.
4. Join the points to get the cumulative frequency curve. Cumulative frequency curve can be smoothed in the same manner that frequency polygon can be smoothed.

The Cumulative Percentage Curve or Ogive

The cumulative percentage curve or ogive differs from cumulative frequency curve in that frequencies are expressed as cumulative percents of frequency on the X-axis. In table 6 cumulative frequencies have been converted into cumulative percents.

The procedure of plotting ogive is exactly the same as that of plotting cumulative frequency curve except that instead of cumulative frequencies, the percentages of cumulative frequencies are plotted on the upper exact limits of the class interval.

Example : Plot an ogive of the distribution given in table 7.

Step 1. Find out the exact upper limits of each class interval.

Step 2. Accumulate the successive frequencies.

Step 3. Convert these cumulated frequencies into percentage to obtain cumulative percentage.

Step 4. Plot these cumulative percentage on the upper exact limits of the class intervals in the same manner as we have done in case of plotting of cumulative frequency curve. The only difference is that on the Y-axis instead of cumulative frequencies cumulative percentage frequencies are marked off from 0 to 100.

Step 5. Join the points smoothly to get ogive freehand.

TABLE 6 : **Cumulative percentage frequencies**

Class interval	*Upper exact limits*	*X*	*Cumulative frequency (c.f.)*	*Percentage cumulative frequency % (c.f.)*
41-43	43.5	1	86	100.0
38-40	40.5	4	85	98.8
35-37	37.5	5	81	94.2
32-34	34.5	8	76	88.4
29-31	31.5	14	68	79.1
26-28	28.5	17	54	62.8
23-25	25.5	9	37	43.0
20-22	22.5	13	28	32.6
17-19	19.5	8	15	17.4
14-16	16.5	3	7	8.1
11-13	13.5	4	4	4.7
8-10	10.5	0	0	00.0

When to use the Frequency Polygon and Histogram

The frequency Polygon is less precise than the histogram because it does not represent accurately in terms of area, the frequency in each interval. In comparing two or more graphs plotted on the same axis, the frequency polygon is likely to be more useful.

MEASURES OF CENTRAL TENDENCY

There are three methods commonly used for the measure of centred tendency.

(a) The arithematic mean or simple means (b) The median (c) The mode

The Arithematic Mean : The Arithmetic mean is the most familiar and most frequently used measure of central tendency. It is relatively easy to use this method for measurement of central tendency. This term is usually implied where mean is used without a modifier. Arithmetic mean or simple mean is obtained by adding all the values and dividing the total by the number of values. If X denotes the measurement then the mean is always denoted by $\bar{X}$ (X bar) or N, and if N stands for the number of values and symbol (sigma) denotes the sum of all the terms then we have the formula :

$$M \text{ or } X = \frac{\Sigma X}{N}$$

$$i.e., \quad \text{Mean} = \frac{\text{Sum of the scores of values}}{\text{Number of score or values}}$$

e.g. —1. The following are the ungrouped score of 8 students ;
49, 54, 53, 52, 55, 53, 57, 51

Calculate mean score.

Sol. By definition, the mean

$$M = \frac{\Sigma X}{N} \text{ or } M = \bar{X} = \frac{49+54+53+52+55+53+57+51}{8}$$

$$= \frac{424}{8} = 52.62$$

Deviation

Deviation of any value X from its mean is its differences with the mean. In the above example the deviation of 54 from its mean 53 is 1, *i e.*, (54−53)=1; similarly the deviation of 49 from its mean is −4 *i.e.* (49−53).

Hence we can say deviation = Score − Mean

$$X = X - M$$

where X denotes deviation of Score X from its true mean.

Short Method of Calculating the Mean

In this method first an arbutary (assumed) working mean and calculate the deviations of the observations from this workink mean. If X denotes deviation of value X from assumed mean A.M.

$$X = X - A.M.$$

$$M = \bar{X} = A.M. + \frac{\Sigma X}{N}$$

TABLE 7

Serial No.	*X*	*X=X—52*
1	49	—3
2	54	2
3	53	1
4	52	0
5	55	3
6	53	1
7	51	2
8	54	—1
		ΣX=+5'

To obtain the accurate final result, any assumed mean will do, but the reduce computation, care should be taken to select the assumed mean as possible to the actual mean.

The Arithmatic Mean of Grouped Data

To calculate Mean of Grouped data we can apply the formula.

$$M = \frac{\Sigma fx}{N}$$

Where Σ fx is the sum of produet of frequency (f) and the mid point (X) of class interval.

Step 1—Find out the mid point of each class interval by finding out the average of the upper and lower scores of class.

Step 2—To obtain the value of fx multiply each mid-point value (x) by the frequency.

Step—3 Add all the value of fx to obtain Σ fx.

Step—4 Apply the formula

$$M = \frac{\Sigma fx}{N}$$

This will give us the value of mean.

Example : From the given frequency distribution, calculate the values of mean.

TABLE 8

Score	*X*
34-38	3
30-34	2
25-29	2
20-24	5
15-19	6
10-14	4
5-9	1

N=23

Solution

Score	*Mid-points of the interval (X)*	(*f*)	(*fx*)
34-38	36	3	108
30-34	32	2	64
25-29	27	2	54
20-24	22	5	110
15-19	17	6	102
10-14	12	4	48
5-9	7	1	7
		N=23	Σ fx=493

$$M = \frac{\Sigma fx}{N} = \frac{493}{23} = 21.43$$

Arithmetic Mean from Group data (Short method) :

The steps in the process of computing mean from frequency distribution by the short cut method is as follows:

Step 1. All the data of the frequency distribution are arranged than added to get the total number of items *i.e.* N=Σ and width of class interval is found out.

Step 2. By inspection the interval in the distribution which is most likely to contain mean is estimated. And the midpoint of this interval will be designated AM formula.

Step 3. In the fourth column *i.e.* the one which is next to that of frequencies, the deviation x′ of the mid-point of the interval from the assumed mean in steps is marked *i.e.* those values greater than the assumed mean are designated as (+) and those lesser are designated as (−)

Step 4. Each frequency (f) is multiplied by its corresponding deviation (x′). The products (fx′) are then written in the fifth column. Care regarding sign's should be taken.

Step 5. Algebraic sum of fx′ (Σ fx′) is calculated from fifth column.

Step 6. The value of fx′ is then divided by N. Sometimes fx′ will be positive and sometimes negative. There sign will depend on the position of assumed mean.

Step 7. $\frac{fx'}{N}$ is then multiplied by the size of the class interval. The size of the class interval is also called width of the class interval and this is equal to the difference between lower or upper limits of two consecutive class intervals.

Step 8. The final step is to find the algebraic sum of A.M. and

$$\frac{fx'}{N} \times i$$

$$\text{Thus } M = \bar{X} = A.M. + \frac{fx'}{N} \times i$$

When all the classes are of equal width then this formula is applicable.

TABLE 9

Class Interval Scores	*Mid-point*	*f*	*x*	*fx'*
195-199	197	1	5	5
190-194	192	2	4	8
185-189	187	4	3	12
180-184	182	5	2	10
175-179	177	8	1	8
				+43
170-174	172	10	0	
165-169	167	6	−1	−6
160-164	162	4	−2	−8
155-159	157	4	−3	−12
150-154	152	2	−4	−8
145-149	147	3	−5	−15
140-144	142	1	−6	−6
		N=50		−55

A.M. = 172.00

i. = 5

N = 50

$\Sigma fx' = +43 - 55 = -12$

$$\text{Mean} = \text{A.M.} + \frac{\Sigma fx'}{N} \times i$$

$$= 172 + \frac{(-12)}{50} \times 5$$

$$= 172 + (-.240) \times 5.$$

$$= 172 + (-1.20)$$

$$= 170.80$$

Mean from Combined samples of groups : Suppose that on a certain test the mean from a group of 40 children is 66. Less the mean of the two groups combined is $\frac{62 \times 10 + 66 \times 40}{50} = 66$

The formula for the weighted mean of n group is

$$M\ comb = \frac{N_1M_1 + N_2M_2 + \dots\dots\dots N_nM_n}{N_1 + N_2 + \dots\dots\dots N_n}$$

(Weighted with arithmetical mean obtained from combining) n groups).

When only two groups are combined the weighted mean formula becomes

$$M\ comb = \frac{N_1M_1+N_2M_2}{N_1+N_2}$$

When to Use the Mean

(i) When the scores distributed symmetrically around a central point, *i.e.*, when the distribution is not badly skewed. The M is the centre of gravity in the distribution and each score contributes to its determination.

2. When the measure of central tendency having the greatest stability is wanted.

3. When other statistics (leg) S.D., coefficient of correlation are to be computed later. Many statistics are based upon the mean.

Median

Mostly arithmetic mean is used to summarise the general character of data. But if the collection of Data contains extreme values, which effect the arithmetic mean the arithmetic mean is in appropriate. For example if the sample of five values is 45, 57, 65, 90, 68 its arithmetic mean is 71.0. This value is not the time representative of the sample. Thus in such cases another value called median is used.

Median of a set of data is that point below and above which 50% of the value lie. It is the half way mark when data are ranked (arranged in order of magnitude). In the above example values are in ascending order and the middle value is 65. Therefore, the median is 65. Median does not take into consideration the absolute difference in successive pairs of values. The median is also called position average. In arithmetic mean each value contributes to the final result according to the magnitude. In median only the middle value represents the whole data.

If the series consists of an old number of values the median is the middle value.

If the series consist of an even number of values, the median is assumed to fall midway between the two middle values after the series is arranged in the numerical order *i.e.*, it is arithemetic mean of two middle values. For example median of 31, 32, 35, 36, 38 and 42 is $\frac{35+36}{2}=35.5$.

Calculation of Median for Grouped Data

In case of grouped data *i.e.*, frequency distribution firstly cumulative frequency distribution and then the formula for calculating median is

$$\text{Mdn}=l+\frac{(N/2-F)}{f}\times i$$

Where Mdn is median, l is the exact lower limit of the interval which contains the median, the point below which half number of cases lie, i is the width of the class interval in which the median falls, f is the frequency of the same interval and F is the cumulative frequency of the preceding classes.

Q. **Example**—Calculate median from the data given in Table 10.

TABLE 10

C.I.	*f*
70-71	2
68-69	2
66-67	3
64-65	4
62-63	6
60-61	7
58-59	5
56-57	4
54-55	2
52-53	3
50-51	5
	N=40

Solution

Step 1. We first add the frequencies and get N=40.

Step 2. As we have working formula for the median as

$$\text{Mdn}=l+\frac{(N/2-F)}{f}\times i$$

We need (the exact lower limit of the median class) and F, (the cumulative frequency) *i.e.* c.f. of the preceding class.

Step 3. Then we take the exact limits and prepare a cumulative frequency distribution.

Step 4. We thus get the following table 5.

Step 5. Here N=40 therefore $\frac{N}{2}=\frac{40}{2}=20$. Hence the median class (class in which the median lies) is 60-61.
Step 6 Calculation

$$\text{Mdn}=1+\frac{(N/2-F)}{F}\times i$$

Here 1=the exact lower limit of the C.I. '60-61' is 59.5

TABLE 11

C.I.	*f*	*c.f.*
70-71	2	40
68-69	2	38
66-67	3	36
64-65	4	33
62-63	6	29
60-61	7	23
58-59	5	16
56-57	4	11
54-55	2	7
52-53	3	5
50-51	2	2
	N=40	

F=16 (cumulative frequency preceding C.I. (60-61)

F=7 (frequency in the Mdn class).

Putting the value, we get

$$\text{Median}=\frac{N}{2}-F$$

$$\text{Median}=1+\frac{\qquad}{F}\times i$$

$$=59.2+\frac{20-16}{7}\times 2$$

$$=59.5+4\times\frac{4}{7}\times 2$$

$$=59.5+1.14$$

$$=60.64$$

Calculation of the Median When

(a) The frequency distribution contains gaps ; and

(b) The first or last interval has indeterminate limits.

a. When there are gaps limits among one or more frequency intervals.

Example

TABLE 12

C.I.	*f*	*C.f.*
20-21	2	16
18-19	2	14
16-17	4	12
14-15	0	8
12-13	4	8
10-11	0	4
8-9	4	4
N=16		

Now N=16, N/2=1 which is the cf in both the c.'s of (12-13) and (14-15) giving the two values of median, if ordinary method is applied median may be either 15.5 or 13.5. Similarly there are cases where more than two such values are obtained (if there are many zero frequencies). There are many ways of adjusting these cases. One of the easiest ways is to take the mean of the exact lower limit of the first and the upper limit of the last cases interval in which cumulative frequency is N/2. In this case c.f.=N/2 in (12-13) and (14-15). The mean of 11.5 and 15.5 is 13.5. Hence median here is 13.5.

(b) The mean of grouped data cannot be calculated, if the distribution is open ended (*e.g.* 80 and above at the higher end or '20 and below, after lowest end) but the median is readily computed because each score is simply contend as one frequency whether accurately classified or not, provided that the class in which median falls is defined.

When to Use the Median

(1) When the exact midpoint of the distribution is wanted the 50% point.

(2) When there are extreme scores which would markedly affect the mean. Extreme scores do not disturb the median. For example in series 4, 5, 6, 7 and 8 both mean and median are 6. But if 8 is replaced by 60 the other scores remaining the same, the median is still 6 but the mean is 14.4.

(3) When it is desired that certain scores should influence the central tendency, but all that is known about them is that they are above or below the median.

Mode

The mode is the value of the variate that occurs most commonly *i.e.* that value of variate for which frequency is maximum. If one value oecurs maximum number of times then the distribution is said to be unimodal. On the other hand, if more than one value is repeated mostly the distribution is said to be multifolded.

Mode is the most representative of observations because it tells us that which value is most common. But difficulties arise in the calculation of this value. If each value of the variate has same frequency (rectangular or uniform) the mode has no meaning. This is greatly influenced by the width of the class interval used in grouping.

If the distribution is unimodal there is hardly any difficulty in calculation.

Example 4 : Find the mode of the following observations

1, 2, 5, 3, 5, 4, 4, 5, 6, 3, 6

Solution

In this the distribution is unimodal and 5 occurs maximum number of times. Therefore the mode is 5.

Calculation of Mode for Grouped Data

In the grouped data the crude mode is the midpoint of the

class interval, while the mode is calculated by following formula.

Mode=3 Median−2 Mean

(i) **Calculation of Mode Directly**

Mode can be calculated by the following formula.

$$M_0 = l + \left(\frac{(f_1 - F_0)}{2f_i - f_0 - f_2} \right) \times i$$

Where l=lower exact limit of the model class

fi=frequency of the model class.

f_0=frequency of the class preceding the model class.

f_2=frequency of the class succeeding the model class

i=class interval

Example—Calculate mode from the following frequency distribution.

TABLE 13

Score	*f*
35-39	1
30-34	2
25-29	4
20-24	6
15-19	1
10-14	1
	N=15

Solution—First step is to identify the model class *i.e.* the class having highest frequency. In the above examples by inspection we see that mode lies in the class 20-24. Second step is to apply the formula.

$$M_0 = l + \frac{(f_1 - f_0)}{2\,f_1 - f_0 - f_2} \times i$$

$$l=19.3$$

$$f_1=6$$

$$f_0=1$$

$$f_2=4$$

$$i=5$$

$$=19.5+\frac{(6-1)}{2\times 6-1-4}\times 5$$

$$=19.5+\frac{5}{12-5}\times 5$$

$$=19.5+\frac{25}{7}$$

$$=19.5+3.57$$

$$=23.07$$

(ii) **Calculation of Mode from Mean and Median Values (Grouped data).**

TABLE 14

Scores	*f*
90-94	2
85-89	2
80-84	4
75-79	8
70-74	8
65-69	12
60-64	9
55-59	7
50-54	5
45-49	1
40-44	2

(ii) Calculation of mean

TABLE 1

Scores	F	dorx1	fd or fx1
90-94	2	+5	10
85-89	2	+4	8
80-84	4	+3	12
75-79	8	+2	16
70-74	8	+1	8
65-69	12	0	0+54
60-64	9	−1	−9
55-59	7	−2	−14
50-54	5	−3	−15
45-49	1	−4	−4
40-44	2	−5	−10
			−52
			$\Sigma fx^1 = 2$ or Σfd

$$\text{Mean} = \text{AM} + \frac{\Sigma fx^1}{N} \times i$$

$$= 67 + \frac{2}{60} \times 5$$

$$= 67 + .16$$

$$= 67.16$$

(ii) Calculation of median

TABLE 16

Scores	f	c.f.
90-94	2	60
85-89	2	58
80-84	4	56
75-79	8	52
70-74	8	44
65-69	12	36
60-64	9	24
55-59	7	15
50-54	5	8
45-49	1	3
40-44	2	2

$$\text{Median} = l + \frac{\frac{N}{2} - F}{f} \times i$$

$$= 64.5 + \frac{30-24}{12} \times 5$$

$$= 64.5 + \frac{6}{12} \times 5$$

$$= 64.5 + \frac{30}{12}$$

$$= 64.5 + 2.5$$

$$= 67$$

Calculation of Mode—

$$\text{Mode} = 3 \text{ Median} - 2 \text{ Mean}$$

$$3 \times 67 = 2 \times 67.16$$

$$201 - 134.32$$

$$= 66.68$$

When We Use the Mode

1. When a quick and approximate measure of central tendency is all that is wanted.
2. When the measure of central tendency should be the most typical value. When we describe the style of dress or shoes worn by the "average woman", for instance, the model or most popular fashion is usually meant. In like manner, in speaking of the average wage in a certain industry, we often mean the model wage under specified conditions.

MEASURES OF VARIABILITY

Introduction

Central tendencies are central values which the individual observations are distributed. They give us an idea of location of the distribution, but tell us nothing as to how the individual scores are scattered. Thus each of the following six series, has 5 as the mean although the patterns of individual measurements are different series.

(i) 5 5 5 5 5 5

(ii) 3 4 5 6 7

(iii) 2 3 4 6 7 8

(iv) 0 9 2 2 2 3 4 26

(v) 1 9

(vi) 4.5 5 5.5

Thus we observe that measurement of central tendency alone is not example ; we should also know how the individual scores are clustered around or scattered away from the central value. This characteristic of distribution is called variability, dispersion or the spread.

Measurement of Variability

The following are main measures of variability or dispersion of the individual observations in the population :

1. *Range*—The range of a distribution is the difference between the maximum and minimum value of the variate. It is easily calculated. The ranges of the above five series are 0, 4, 6, 26, 8 and 1 respectively. It is readily understood and gives us some idea of the amount of dispersion present, but it is very crude and unstable measures of variability since it depends entirely on two extreme values in the series and indicates virtually nothing about the general form of the series. Therefore, quite frequently range misleads regarding dispersion of the distribution.

2. *Quartile Range*—Another way of describing the dispersion of distribution is in terms of quartile range. In determining this measure 25 percent of lowest values and 25 percent of the upper values are disregarded. If Q_1 is first quartile and Q_3 is third quartile, then Quartile Range$=Q_3$-Q_1. Half of this range is termed as semi-interquartile range or quartile deviation (Q.D or Simple Q). The range and the quartile range both do not take into consideration the value of each individual item of the distribution and therefore, both lack in descriptive value. A good measure of dispersion should depend upon the amounts by which the scores deviate from the measure of central tendency, say mean. Next measure depends upon deviation of each individual item from the mean.

3. *Average Deviation* (*A.D.*)—The average deviation (A.D.) is

mean of the deviation of all the separate scores in a series taken from their mean.

$$A.D. = \frac{\Sigma(X)}{N}$$

where

$\Sigma(x)$ indicates magnitude of deviation by ignoring +ve or —ve sign.

We calculate $X-M=x$ for all the scores and get (x) by disregarding its proper sign (+or —)

Add all the (X) and divide the sum thus obtained by N. An example will make the definition clear. The mean of the 5 scores, 6, 8, 10, 12 and 14 is 10. And the deviations of the separate scores from this mean are 6—10 or —4, 8—10 or —2, 10—10 or 0 ; 12—10 or 2 ; 14—10 or 4. The sum of these 5 deviations, disregarding signs, is 12, and dividing 12 by 5 (N), we get 2.4 as the mean of these 5 deviations from their mean, or the A.D.

Calculation of the A.D. from Grouped Data—The A.D. from grouped data can also be calculated. The deviation of the mid-point of the class-intervals are calculated and multiplied by their respective frequencies. The sum (ignoring the signs) divided by N gives us the required A.D. The formula for the same is

$$A.D. = \Sigma \frac{|F_x|}{N}$$

The A.D. is rarely used in modern statistics, but it is often found in the old experimental literature.

Standard Deviation

Standard Deviation is the square root of the mean of the squares of deviation taken from the mean. It is the positive square root of the mean of the squares of the deviations from the arithmetic mean and it is denoted by a Greek letter σ (sigma) and in short it is called S.D. The standard deviation is the most widely used measure of dispersion.

(1) *Calculation of the S.D. from Ungrouped Scores*—We may illustrate the calculation of the S.D. for an ungrouped set of data with the same 5 scores used in the computation of the A.D. The mean of the 5 scores 6, 8, 10, 12 and 14 is 10 and the deviation of the separate scores from the mean are —4, —2, 0, 2, and 4

respectively. When each of these 5 deviations is squared, we get 16, 4, 0, 4 and 16, the sum is 40 and N, of course, is 5. The formula for σ when scores are ungrouped is

$$\sigma = \sqrt{\frac{\Sigma x^2}{N}}$$

$$\sigma = \sqrt{\frac{40}{5}}$$

$$\sigma = 2.83$$

Calculation of the S.D. from grouped data.

TABLE 17

Short Method

(1) Scores	(2) Mid-point	(3) f	(4) x'	(5) fx'	(6) fx'^2
195-199	197	1	5	5	25
190-194	192	2	4	8	32
185-189	187	4	3	12	36
180-184	182	5	2	10	20
175-179	167	8	1	8(+43)	8
170-174	172	10	0	—	
165-169	167	6	—1	—6	6
160-164	162	4	—2	—8	15
155-159	157	4	—3	—12	36
150-154	152	2	—4	—8	32
145-149	157	3	—5	—15	75
140-144	142	1	—6	—6	36
		N=50		98	322 (−55)

A.D. = 172.00 $\quad C = \frac{-12}{50} = -.240$

$C_i = -1.20 \quad C^2 = .0576$

$C_i = -.240 \times 5 = -1.20$

$$\text{S.D.} = i\sqrt{\frac{\Sigma fx'^2}{N} - C^2}$$

$$= 5\sqrt{\frac{322}{50} - .0576}$$

$$= 12.63$$

TABLE 18

2. Long Method

(1) *Scores*	(2) *Mid point*	(3) *f*	(4) *fx*	(5) *x*	(6) *fx*	(7) *fx²*
195-199	197	1	197	26.20	26.20	686.44
190-194	192	2	384	21.20	42.40	898.88
185-189	187	4	748	16.20	64.80	1049.76
180-184	182	5	910	11.20	56.00	627.20
175-179	177	8	1416	6.20	49.60	307.52
170-174	172	10	1720	1.20	12.00	14.40
165-169	167	6	1002	—3.80	—22.80	86.64
160-164	162	4	648	—8.80	—35.20	309.76
155-159	157	4	628	—13.80	—55.20	761.76
150-154	152	2	304	—18.80	—37.60	706.88
145-149	147	3	441	—23.80	—71.40	1699.32
140-144	142	1	142	—28.80	—28.80	829.44
		N=50	8540		502.00	7978.00

1. $M = \frac{\Sigma fx}{N} = \frac{8540}{50} = 170.80$

2. $S.D. = \sqrt{\frac{\Sigma fx^2}{N}}$

$= \sqrt{\frac{7978.00}{50}}$

$= 12.63$

Uses and Characteristics of the Measures of Variability

The Standard Deviation is the most commonly used measure of dispersion. The range and quartile range though simple in calculation are based on only two out of the whole bulk of observations. Moreover, the range of a small sample will not agree well with the range of the distribution from which it is drawn. But on the other hand, S.D. is based on all the observations and is rigidly defined. In some applications of statistics, range is useful as in quality control. But in education, range and quartile range are seldom useful. In fact, none of the measures of dispersion is as useful as the S.D. Most of the methods of statistical analysis have been evolved round the S.D. and its square.

We use the standard deviation in the following situations when—

(a) The greatest dependability of the measure is required.
(b) Further calculations that depend upon it are likely to be needed.
(c) Interpretations related to normal distribution curve are to be done.

Variance

The term variance is used to denote the square of the standard deviation *i.e.* ^{2}

We have

$$V(x)=\sigma^2=\frac{\Sigma(x-M)^2}{N}$$

Use of Measures of Variability

The following general rules will serve as a useful guide for the use of the various measures of variability.

(1) *Use of Range*

(i) When the data are too scant or too scattered to justify the computation of a more precise measure of variability.
(ii) When knowledge of extreme scores or of total spread is all that is wanted.

(2) *Use of Q*

(i) When the median is the measure of central tendency.
(ii) When there are extreme scores which have disproportionate influence on S.D.
(iii) When the concenttration around median is of primary interest (*i.e.* mid cases).
(iv) When the upper and lower class intervals are open.

(3) *Use of A.D.*

(i) When it is desired to weight all deviations from the mean according to their size.

(ii) When extreme deviations would influence S.D. unduly.

(4) *Use of S.D.*

(i) When the statistic having the greatest stability is sought.

(ii) When extreme deviations should exercise a proportionally greater effect upon the variability.

(iii) When co-efficients of correlation and other statistics are subsequently to be computed.

PERCENTILE OR PERCENTILE RANKS

Introduction

It is based on the order or ranking of scores. In a set of scores, 60, 95, 72, 80, 83, 90, 76 and 66 a typical score which falls in the middle of the scale of measurement describes the characteristic of performance of the group. Arranging the data in an ascending order or magnitude in the following way.

60, 66, 72, 76, 80, 83, 90, 96 the median (middle score) *i.e.* (76+80)/2=78 may be obtained. Some other typical positions of a series may be found.

Quartiles

These are the points which divide the scale of measurement

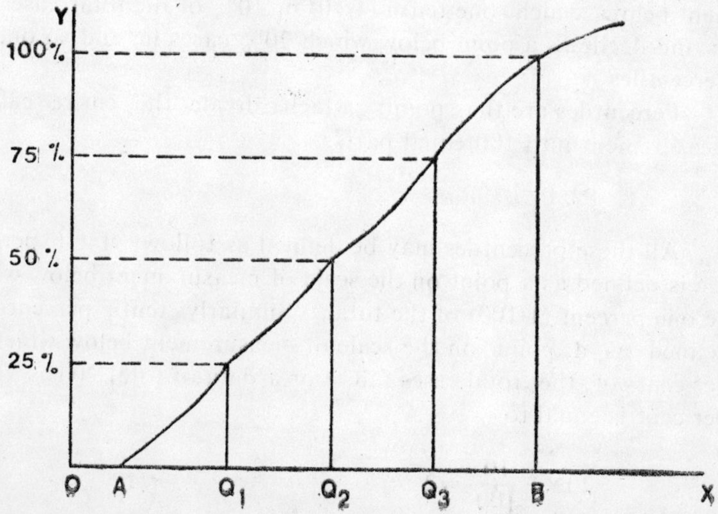

into four equal parts. To divide a series in four equal parts we have to drain in ogive and divide it into points below, which 25%, 50%, 75% and 100% cases be. These are known as first quartile (Q_1), second quartile (Q_2) third quartile (Q_3) and fourth quartile (Q_4) respectively.

Deciles

These are the points which divide the scale of measurement into ten equal parts.

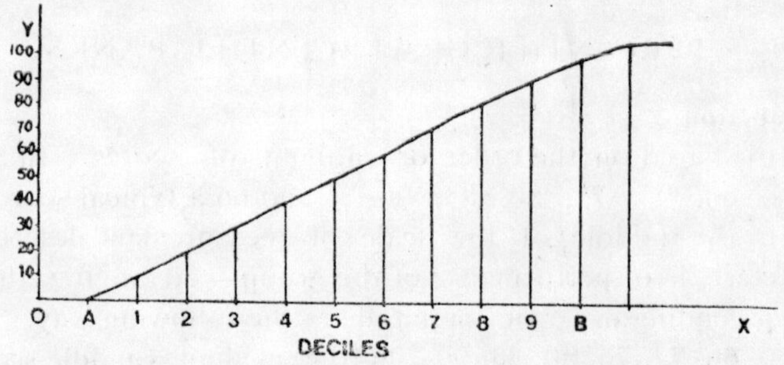

Thus there will be in all ten deciles *viz.* first decile to ninth decile. These deciles are denoted by D_1, D_2, D_3, D_4.........D_2, D_{10}.

First decile is defined as the point on the scale of measurement below which one-tenth (1/10) or 10% of the total cases lie, second decile as a point below which 20% cases lie and so on.

Percentiles

Percentiles are the points which divide the entire scale of measurement into 100 equal parts.

P_1, P_2......P_{100}

All these percentiles may be defined as follow. First percentile is defined as a point on the scale of measurement below which lie one percent (1/100) of the total. Similarly tenth percentile is defined as a point on the scale of measurement below which 10 per cent of the total cases fall. For a data of total 20 cases, ten per cent is equal to

$$20 \times \frac{10}{100} = 2$$

Quartiles

P_{25}, the score below which 25% of the cases lie is called the first or lower quartile and is denoted by the symbol Q_1. In the following example 25% of students *i.e.* 5 students lie below a point between 36 and 40.

Ex. 1. 95, 85, 80, 78, 75, 62, 60, 60, 60, 54, 50, 50, 48, 45, 40, 36, 32, 31, 30, 25

Hence $Q_1 = P_{25} = 1/2\ (36+40) = 38$

Similarly, P_{75} is the score below which 75% of the cases lie is called the third or upper quartile and is denoted by the symbol Q_3.

In the last example below Q_3 score of 15 students should lie and therefore Q_3 lies between 62 and 75.

$$Q_3 = P_{75} = 68.5$$

The difference between Q_1 and Q_3 known as inter-quartile range

$$Q_3 - Q_1 = 68.5 - 38$$

$$30.5$$

Percentile for frequency distribution

To calculate it we first find cumulative frequency for each class. This gives the number of cases below each score.

Ex. 2. Following is the distribution of scores on a test of class of 40 students.

In the next table cumulative frequency is found by adding each frequency to the total of the frequencies.

P_{25} will be a score below which 25% *i.e.* 10 students lie. From the column of cumulative frequency we found that 10 students be below 3.5. Therefore $P_{25} = 3.5$, $P_{75} = 6.5$.

TABLE 19

1 Score x	*2* Frequency f	*3* Cumulative frequency Cf (F)
10	1	40
9	2	39
8	3	37
7	4	34
6	5	30
5	8	25
4	7	17
3	3	10
2	3	7
1	3	4
0	1	1

$$P_x = l + \frac{\left(\frac{xN}{100} - F\right)}{f} \times i$$

where l=is the power limit of the class interval in which Px falls.

N=The total frequencies

F=cumulative frequency immediately below l

f=the frequency of the class interval in which px falls.

i=size of the class interval in which p_x falls.

Ex. Calculate P_{10}, P_{25}, P_{50}, P_{75} from the following table of frequency distribution.

TABLE 20

1 Class interval	*2* (*f*)	*3* Cf
120-139	50	1000
100-119	150	950
80-99	500	800
60-79	250	300
40-59	50	50
	N=1000	

$$\frac{xN}{100} = P_n$$

Calculation—$P_x = 1 + \frac{P_n - F}{f} \times i$

$P_{10} = 10\%$ of $1000 = 100$

$59.5 + \frac{100 - 50}{250} \times 20$

$= 63.5$

$P_{25} = 25\%$ of $1000 = 250$

$59.5 + \frac{250 - 50}{250} \times 20$

$= 75.5$

$P_{50} = 50\%$ of $1000 = 500$

$79.5 + \frac{500 - 300 \times 20}{500}$

$= 87.5$

$P_{75} = 75\%$ of $1000 = 750$

$79.5 + \frac{750 - 300}{500} \times 20$

$= 97.5$

Steps to calculate a percentile :

For calculating Xth precentile the following steps should be taken—

1. Cumulative frequency is computed for the given frequency distribution.

2. Compute a fraction $= \frac{XN}{100}$, and the class in which p_x falls is calculated. It is a class where the value of cumulative frequency associated with a class just exceeds the value of the fraction $\frac{XN}{100}$.

3. Determine the value of l, f, F and i.

4. These Numerical values which are stated above are put in formula and results are obtained.